Women Managers

Changing Organizational Cultures

Gisèle Asplund

GA Konsult AB

JOHN WILEY & SONS
Chichester · New York · Brisbane · Toronto · Singapore

Copyright © 1988 by John Wiley & Sons Ltd.

All rights reserved.

No part of this book may be reproduced by any means, or transmitted, or translated into a machine language without the written permission of the publisher.

$34.95

Library of Congress Cataloging in Publication Data:

Asplund, Gisèle, 1943–
  Women managers.

  Includes index.
  1. Women executives—Sweden.   2. Corporate culture—Sweden.   3. Leadership.   I. Title.
  HD6054.4.S8A775   1988   302.3′5   88-10801
ISBN 0 471 91292 1

British Library Cataloguing in Publication Data available

  ISBN 0 471 91292 1

Printed and bound in Great Britain by Biddles of Guildford

DEDICATION

To my children
Louise and Daniel.

*Vision, courage
and good luck!*

CONTENTS

PREFACE

This is a book about men, women and leadership. During the last 15 years many things have happened in the labour market. In all Western Countries women have progressed and have enforced their positions in this market and in the economy. For example, in Sweden 50 per cent of the employees are now women. However, they are still in lower positions and do not have the same salaries as men, even when they have had the same education.

Much of the research in the 1970s and early 1980s was concerned with descriptive data. What jobs did women actually have? Why? Was there a connection between low-salaried jobs and women's traditional housework? Eventually the focus of research turned to leadership questions. Leadership styles and the communication between male superiors and female subordinates was evaluated, and many studies showed that this communication was not always effective. This was used as one of the explanations of why women failed to climb the hierarchical ladder.

I was working as an organizational consultant in the late 1970s and the early 1980s. In many of the organizations I studied I saw the same picture. Women at the bottom of the hierarchy felt frustrated and did not understand why they progressed so slowly! I organized a project in five large companies: a bank, an insurance company, two manufacturers and a government agency. I used both a sociological and a psychological approach, sent a questionnaire to 2000 women and men and had extensive interviews with a sample of about 50 men and women (in the same organizations). A detailed explanation of the methods used is given in the Methodological Appendix at the end of this book.

My conclusions of this work lead me to believe that some of the prevailing 'myths' are true while others are not. For example, women are career orientated to the same degree as men *but* they experience more hindrances and problems. On many occasions they also feel a lack of support from male bosses. However, in organizations where the culture is effective and truly goal-oriented, women do have the same opportunities as men.

There are still very few women in high leadership positions, and it is difficult to prove that they can add something to organizational culture just because they happen to be women. However, when given the chance of taking high risks and important management decisions—thereby using their leadership talent— women have shown that they are fully competent to fulfil this task.

GISÈLE ASPLUND

Stockholm December 1987

Chapter 1

WOMEN MANAGERS —WHY SO FEW?

1.1 WOMEN MANAGERS AND DECISION-MAKERS

Many women in Western Europe work outside the home but very few are managers. Even in Sweden, which is generally regarded as a progressive country, the truth of this statement is all too obvious. Women managers are more common in the public sector than in the private, particularly in public administration, but even here the numbers of women in managerial positions is fewer than it should be in relation to the total number of female employees. Even in organizations with a predominantly female staff, very few of the women are managers. At the Swedish Central Bureau of Statistics, for example, roughly 7 per cent of the women (as against 20 per cent of the men) are in positions involving any kind of managerial function, although almost half the staff is female. Of the 2 million women working in Sweden the majority are employed in the public sector.

Thus women are underrepresented in the private sector as a whole, and within this sector women and men predominate in different branches of industry. Almost 50 per cent of males working in the private sector are in the manufacturing industry; the equivalent figure for women is 30 per cent. This segregation emerges even more clearly when we breakdown the figures for different trades. Women predominate primarily in food, the graphics industry, and electrical manufacturing, and men in machine engineering, wood products, paper pulp, and the metal industries.

However, women are not simply concentrated in certain sectors or industries; their distribution in the position hierarchy also differs greatly from that of men.

Women do advance up the corporate ladder but their progress is hardly rapid. Recent international surveys show that women in Europe and the United States occupy about 2 per cent of all senior executive positions. In Sweden such women are to be found

3

mainly in areas such as personnel, information and education. At present there is only one woman in Sweden who is managing director of a stock-exchange listed company, Lena Vennberg, a journalist and economist who previously made a career for herself in the Swedish Broadcasting Corporation.

Thus progress is slow, but we must bear in mind that although it takes a good 10–15 years to reach the level immediately below the top the near future looks promising; this is because Sweden now has many more women in middle-management positions than, for instance, in the 1970s.

With middle-management positions it is difficult to make international comparisons, as each country has its own position nomenclature. However, by combining various criteria such as salaries, education etc. we can arrive at a credible estimate, i.e. that about 15–20 per cent of all middle-management positions are now held by women both in Europe and the United States.

According to *The Economist* (March 1987) only 8.4 per cent of those awarded MBA degrees in 1975 in the United States were women, compared with 30 per cent in 1986. The Swedish figures are approximately the same. All these highly educated women are pressing for a place on the corporate ladder, and I feel fairly sure that within the next ten years we are going to see significant changes in favour of women at the senior executive level.

At this point it seems relevant to examine the role of equal opportunities legislation. Sweden passed a law on equal opportunities in 1980, Japan did not follow until 1986, whereas the United States has had an Equal Opportunities Act in operation since the early 1970s. Japanese women still have a long way to go to reach even middle-management levels, while the United States can probably still be said to have made most progress in this field. However, many European countries are falling behind less than might be expected, considering that their laws are by no means as 'effective' as those in the United States. A comparison between American and Swedish sex-discrimination laws, for instance, reveals that the American law is designed as a minority one (although it is in fact applied to a majority, as women out number men in the United States). According to this law, the public prosecutor can bring an action against any company or organization that fails to pay due consideration to minority representation. The prosecutor will generally examine the situation at different levels in the company, and if opportunities are found to be unacceptably unequal, objectives are set up for correcting the faults.

A well-known case concerned to the privately owned Bell Telephone Company. Here, few women were to be found in the upper strata of the corporate hierarchy, while at lower levels segregation was very evident: repairmen and assembly workers were almost exclusively male and telephone operators almost exclusively female. The company was given a certain number of years in which to correct this, partly by external recruitment but mainly by extensive education and retraining programmes. The intention was not to create a completely symmetrical pyramid with 50 per cent of each sex in all positions but radical changes were called for at every level.

In recent years many American companies have embarked voluntarily on change programmes of this kind, which suggests that the law and the first test cases in the 1970s made a strong impact. A few years ago General Motors was sentenced to allocate $65 million to an equal opportunities campaign, to include long-term training programmes and the payment of compensation to those who had been receiving inequitable wages.

Naturally it is the sanctions permitted by the American legislation, i.e. the extremely high fines, which give weight to the law. Compared with American law, European equal opportunities legislation is but a pale shadow—which does not mean that a law on the American model would be either desirable or possible in

6

Europe. However, there is every reason to try to influence those who underestimate the vital importance of the whole equality issue.

According to Swedish equal opportunities legislation, for instance, women and men should have equal rights as regards work, working conditions, and opportunities for development. The law itself has two main sections. The first of these prohibits any discrimination by sex. No employer may treat an applicant or an employee unfavourably on account of his or her sex. The prohibition is mandatory, but exceptions are made to allow positive discrimination in cases of sex-related underrepresentation. This means that an employer must choose a job applicant belonging to the underrepresented sex, even though he or she may not be the best qualified person. Such an approach is allowed only as part of a specified plan for combating sex-discrimination and for achieving sex equality in certain positions.

The second section of the law lays down rules for ways of achieving equality. It is mandatory for the employer to work purposefully and constructively to this end at his own place of work. For instance, the employer is bound to take positive action to achieve a fair sex distribution within various occupational and personnel categories. Thus, in the light of local conditions he should see that the working environment is appropriate to both women and men. This part of the law is discretionary, i.e. it can be replaced or complemented by collective union agreement. Agreements of this kind may go further than the sex-discrimination law and may be more demanding. The parties on the labour market are then responsible for seeing that the agreement is properly observed.

Where there are no sex-discrimination agreements it is the duty of the Equality Ombudsman to see that the legal requirements for positive action are observed. The public sector, for instance, still lacks many such agreements. Most of the private sector is covered, but the banking system still has no agreement of its own, nor is it alone in this.

According to the law, 'equality' implies equal distribution between men and women within an industry or an occupational category ('equal' here means within the interval 40–60 per cent). It is further required that the two sexes should be equally distributed over all positions and levels in the hierarchy. Thus the intention behind the Swedish law is the same as that behind the American legislation. However, since the Swedish law has no resort to severe penalties of the American type, and since it assumes that the individual must conduct her own case and must prove that she (or, in rare cases, he) has been subject to discrimination, there is very little likelihood of affecting corporate sex equality to any noticeable degree. The resources which have to be allocated by law to training or development activities in American companies must be provided *voluntarily* in Sweden.

Swedish efforts to counter sex discrimination are far more dependent than in many other countries (and certainly than in the United States), on voluntary inputs. However, the fact that there is an Equal Opportunities Act compels employers to pay attention to women in their companies. To put it another way, the laws seem to have a great impact on attitudes to women and have thus been a vital tool for those working for the advancement of women at work.

1.2 HOW DO ORGANIZATIONS WORK?

A little straightforward observation suggests a number of general characteristics which define the 'typical' organization. Despite a certain tendency towards decentralization (for example, the distribution of responsibility for decisions and results among small organizational units), on the subject of *power and decision-*

making the typical organization can still be described as a hierarchy. One of the forces that unites and drives this hierarchy is information.

Anyone who has ever worked in an organization knows that without information one is reduced to the status of an internal exile, excluded and invisible. Of course, the formal or informal *rules* for getting (or being denied) important information are all part of the game: they are moulded by the *norms* obtaining in the organization. However, even if the officially accepted norm states that competence and skill determine promotion, other, less formal, norms such as 'I'll scratch your back if you'll scratch mine' are probably far more potent. This back-scratching norm is extremely common wherever people are forced to compete with one another for a place on the promotion ladder.

Consequently, in the constant struggle to rise in the hierarchy people are eager to be first to learn the rules, to qualify themselves as likely candidates for the next level. Those who command power and information will naturally want something in exchange for supporting 'their' candidate, which is where the 'I'll scratch your back' mechanism often comes into play. The chief executive of a large corporation say: 'If I back you and make you sales manager, then naturally I"ll expect you to back me against the other top managers. And in the power struggle between production and sales which we both know is coming I shall count on your unswerving support.' He may also add: 'And naturally I also know you'll watch your own back, you'll insure us against any unpleasant surprises; your former colleagues will see you've climbed a step or two and will hope for favours from you later on; meanwhile they'll be loyal to us.'

Most people will recognize this description without surprise. Such groups and rivals can be identified everywhere in companies and organizations, extending through successive levels of the hierarchy and even up to the board. However, what we should find surprising—although we probably do not—is the almost total absence of women in such groups. Instead, women lead their own lives on the lower rungs of the ladder, unable, despite their numbers, to force the barrier which seems to appear around the middle of the pyramid and which I call the *promotion bar*.

The promotion bar is a magic frontier which has to be crossed by anyone hoping to compete for the really interesting posts at the top of the tree. The bar is not at the same place in all hierarchies; but anyone working within a particular hierarchy usually knows where it is. In some organizations the bar is strictly and formally defined, as in the civil service, where the promotion path is regulated and specified down to the smallest detail. This probably helps to explain why women have succeeded better in the public sector; in private companies it is often much more difficult to locate the promotion bar and even so difficult to specify the qualifications needed for crossing it. The problem is well illustrated by many advertisements for jobs, where the qualifications for managerial posts are often described in terms of dynamism, energy, vision, fervour, creativity, good judgement, etc. Interviewing the personnel manager of a large company, I once asked why a male candidate had been chosen for a recently advertised job, although at least one woman candidate had appeared very well qualified. I was told 'I felt he had a nose for business'. This was a perfectly serious remark, and I took it as such. Of course, there is something which we call 'a nose for business', but does it always have to be masculine? The fact remains that extremely few women get anywhere near the promotion bar and even fewer cross it. Why?

One explanation, which I have already touched upon, concerns the rules of the game and questions of loyalty. My women readers need only think for a moment. Imagine that you are a man and a manager in a male-dominated hierarchy. Above you, there is nothing but men. It is your job to scan the territory below the promotion bar and to spot potential high-fliers whom you would be prepared to back. Let us also assume that among the candidates are equal numbers of able men and women. Other things being equal, who would you put your money on?

If you choose a man there will be various advantages: you are not breaking with tradition or convention; you know it will not be difficult to teach him, to act as his mentor (after all, you learnt about mentorship from a man yourself). It will also be easy to work with him according to the existing rules of the game.

If you choose a woman there will be all kinds of consequences. The eyes of the world will be on you. 'Why did he do it? Is there something between them? Will he really be able to teach her?' You cannot even travel or have a quiet dinner together. What will your wife or your colleague's husband have to say? If she is pretty, things may be even trickier. You will be on the defensive: 'There's nothing like that about it ...' If she is ugly, people will probably ask: 'What on earth did he pick her up for? With that face she'll scare the customers off.' And so on, *ad infinitum*. However, I can already hear your protests: 'Yes, but that man must be a mass of complexes; I'm not like that. I would ...' That is exactly my point: with a large amount of courage, patience, generosity, humour and insight, you might very well put your money on a woman. However, why should you make such a great effort when we have posited the existence of an equally competent and loyal male candidate whom you could choose without any 'extra' trouble?

I do not see any army of hostile managers, unwilling to encourage women for fear of losing power and prestige; but I do see a great many 'natural' barriers and obstacles *within the hierarchy itself*, in the rules of the game and the norms that determine the rules, all of which help to inhibit the equal opportunities that should be women's by right. It is the facts and myths surrounding this question that chiefly interest me, while I naturally also acknowledge a whole range of other possible reasons for the scarcity of women managers arising from historical and social factors. I shall touch briefly upon some of these below.

1.3 OTHER REASONS FOR THE SCARCITY OF WOMEN MANAGERS

It is important to consider women's role in working life also in a *historical perspective*. Looking at developments over the last few hundred years or so we find that much has happened, both as regards women entering the market for wage labour and the conditions facing them there. Before 1845 Swedish women's inheritance rights were restricted, and before the 1846 freedom of trade reform they had few opportunities for engaging in trade or handicrafts. Not until 1864 were women granted the freedom (at least theoretically) to choose their own professions, and not until the 1870s did university education become open to them. In 1921 Swedish women finally became 'legally responsible persons', and a few years later were granted the right to engage in public service.

In the pre-industrial society (which in Sweden means before about 1870) women outnumbered men in the agricultural sector, while men predominated in most others. During the period up to 1920 there was some increase in women's work. In the early phases of industrialization women accounted for roughly 25–40 per cent of the industrial labour force, but their relative numbers declined successively up to about 1900. Unlike their contemporaries in many other countries, Swedish women did not replace men in industry during the Second World War, and the proportion of women working in industry has remained at around the 20–25 per cent level up to the present.

Another important factor which has affected women's failure

to establish a tradition for themselves in heavy industry in Sweden concerns the *structure* which still characterizes the Swedish economy, with its emphasis on male-dominated industries based on the country's natural resources such as ore and forests. Women have always been more in evidence in industries originating from crafts or from the type of production previously carried on in the home: textiles and clothing, food, leather and the rubber industry. Thus even today women find it difficult to enter the more technological fields that have arisen from the former raw-material-based sectors. In 1983 a report from the Sex Discrimination Ombudsman revealed that even in the new electronics field women appear chiefly in the more humble positions at computer terminals or in traditional roles such as assistants and secretaries.

As well as the more obviously historical factors there are other conditions which have affected women's positions on the labour, market and which I subsume under the composite heading of 'social developments'.

Chief among these factors are, for example, the expansion of the public sector and a variety of social reforms which have made it possible for women to work part time. Perhaps the greatest event for women on the labour market during the 1970s was that each year about 35 000 of them acquired jobs in the local government sector. Many of these women had not previously had jobs at all, but many others were recruited from the private sector. As in industry, the occupations which thus came to be dominated by women tended to belong to the traditionally female domains such as teaching, medical care and so on. In other words, women are building up their own tradition in professional life on the basis of their earlier experience of the caring professions and similar activities which were conducted in the home. The step from this to decision-making positions in industry is, of course, a large one.

The expansion of part-time work is probably another factor blocking women's advancement to supervisory positions, even in sectors where they dominate numerically. Much can—and has been—said about part-time work in this context. From one point of view, part-time work can be claimed as a positive development for women, allowing them to have both a family and a working life. However, part-time work can also hinder a woman's career, since managerial positions call for all her time, while the part-timer is also excluded from further training and other important activities that would help her to mount the career ladder.

The same two-pronged analysis can be directed to all the social benefits which have been developed to help mothers. No other country in the world provides such effective protection during pregnancy, childhood illnesses, etc. as Sweden; at the same time, no women seem to be advancing as slowly towards the top as the Swedish women.

Have these benefits had a recoil effect? Have overprotected women become unwilling to fight for the positions of power? Or has rational economic thinking shown women that, in the short run at least, they lose nothing financially by reducing their working hours? As a result of the Swedish tax system part-time work makes it possible to improve one's quality of life, perhaps by winning more time with the children, while achieving a higher material standard than if one worked full time.

It is also interesting to note that over the last 10 or 15 years the number of self-employed women has been growing. In 1982 women represented almost 30 per cent of the self-employed. This percentage has increased slightly over the last 10 years (from 26.5 per cent to 28.8 per cent), and the four most important branches of industry for women are (1) catering, (2) personal service, (3) retailing, and (4) teaching and medical care, i.e. the same branches of industry which also have a high proportion of women employees.

The interesting point, however, is that we know very little about the reasons for this increase in small female-run businesses, which is just as marked in Europe and the United States as it is in Sweden.

Do women become self-employed because they feel that there will be better opportunities for self-development than there would be in a large company? This is a question to which we have no definite answer at present.

A third type of factor, which may explain the scarcity of women managers at all levels, concerns attitudes and values. There are the psychological and sociological factors. If it is found that women of the right age with the necessary formal training and the right 'spirit' still fail to advance as easily as men, then perhaps there really is a connection with certain attitudes and values embraced by these women, as well as by men, and by the world in which they all work.

Chapter 2

'I WANT TO BE DOING SOMETHING INTERESTING'

2.1 WORK AND EMPLOYMENT

One of the great social issues of the 1980s concerns work and employment. I differentiate between the two concepts because it seems that they refer to substantially different realities. In political debate the words are often used as synonyms, but for most people the associations they evoke are quite different.

Let us consider, for a moment, the associations aroused in us by the following words or sentences:

(1) It is healthy work;
(2) Youth employment schemes are likely to proliferate;
(3) Employment therapy;
(4) Threats to employment.

Is *work* somehow a grander word than *employment*? Although the two terms are used more or less interchangeably in the press and the other media, it seems that 'work' nevertheless has a slightly more dignified and serious ring to it, while 'employment' (or the lack of it) has overtones of an alternative to real work, of jobs created more or less artificially in order to keep people occupied.

Over the last 20 or 30 years there has been a clear shift in trade union focus, at least in the West, as a result of the new situation on the labour market. Trade unions which formerly fought for *shorter working hours* and statutory holidays are now concerned primarily to fight unemployment or, in other words, for the right to *full-time work*.

How has it come about in less than a hundred years that our own knowledge has apparently become a threat to our jobs, so that the problem is now to find meaningful work for all those who want it? Almost everyone seems to!

In discussing these topics young people are quick to express their eagerness 'to get a job and be independent'. They may be pleased enough with a temporary job or a training course, but the most important thing still seems to be to prove to themselves and—even more importantly—to others that they *are* someone, that they have a *job*.

So, what is 'work'? What is a 'job'? The definitions do not seem to be linked exclusively to the idea of physical survival; work also appears to have a value of its own.

In the light of all this it could be interesting to see what differences men and women reveal in their attitudes to work. That there are such differences became clear to me in a series of studies which I shall be describing below.

2.2 'I WANT TO BE DOING SOMETHING INTERESTING'

'I want to be doing something interesting. That's the most important thing for me, if I'm to enjoy my job. But having *a career* isn't my line.' Thus speaks a woman. 'Of course I want *a career*. But I haven't altogether succeeded, I haven't got as far as I'd like.' 'Obviously I aimed at *a career*. I've always wanted to test myself, to see what I'm worth.' The two last quotations are from men.

In interview after interview I discovered the same pattern: *women want to do something interesting, men want a career*. Even women who had a career, who had reached middle-management level, for instance, denied any conscious effort on their own part to achieve their present positions. They explained their 'careers' in terms of chance, the luck of the draw; many of them even seemed slightly embarrassed to talk about their success. A common response would be on the lines of 'Well, I'm actually manager here now, but I don't know whether you can really call it a career. That doesn't sound so good, somehow; and anyway it was just chance that got me the job—I was actually rather surprised to be asked.'

How should we explain this? Does the idea of a career strike men and women in different ways? Do women think that 'doing something interesting', like 'work' in the argument above, sounds in some way morally right, while the whole idea of a career has overtones of 'climbing', 'pushiness', 'competitiveness' etc? Do men have a broader view of their jobs, seeing them as a whole rather than as a series of different things to do? To men, is the idea of 'doing something' also linked to the notion of winning, getting on, having a career?

The existence of sex-related differences in approach was confirmed by the results of three extensive workplace investigations, in which I interviewed men and women who had worked for more than 10 years in the same company or organization. The study included one large private company, one public agency, and one state-owned enterprise. I wanted to see how women and men had succeeded in the same setting over a fairly long period (hence the 10-year criterion), and whether there were any systematic differences in their own perception of their success or failure to get where they wanted.

It may be objected that at the beginning of a career a person probably ought to move about, and this is, of course, correct. However, it still seems that unless someone is recruited externally straight into a managerial post, it takes roughly 10 years to achieve major promotion. Conversely, if after 10 years someone has failed to climb at least a few rungs up the ladder, then that person is probably never going to get on. The three studies will be described in the following section.

2.3 DIFFERENCES IN MEN'S AND WOMEN'S CAREERS

In the interviews I concentrated on a few key topics, i.e.:

(1) When, how, and why the subject had joined the organization;
(2) At what intervals the 'jumps' in their careers had occurred and what these were;
(3) Who had supported or hindered them since they joined the organization;
(4) What was their level of ambition, then and now;
(5) What motivated them or spurred them on;
(6) How they saw their futures;
(7) What contacts they had and what information came their way.

I interviewed people who had risen in the hierarchy and others who had not. There were some clear differences in the attitudes of these two groups, but the greatest emerged from a comparison between male and female subjects.

2.4 WOMEN'S CHOICES ARE LESS CONSCIOUS THAN THOSE OF MEN

At the very first question, concerning people's reasons for joining the particular organization, clear differences emerged. Many women explained that they had not consciously chosen the organization for any particular reason. They had generally tried for several jobs, and as soon as they got any response they had accepted thankfully, without giving the matter much more thought. The fear of not having any job at all was often so strong among the women that even the highly educated ones resigned themselves gratefully to jobs that were well beneath their level of competence and potential. The following are fairly typical as explanations and justifications of job choice.

'I realized this job was beneath me. Sitting as a temp in the purchasing department—I didn't need my education for that. But I consoled myself that at least I'd got a foot in the door of a large successful company, and I thought that when the temp's job was finished, they'd have discovered how good I really was and would offer me something better.'

CHRISTINA, 31, *Economist*

'When I'd got my degree, I didn't know what to do. I'd married a man who was going to move round on the legal circuit. It was simply a matter of tagging along, and for a year or so that's what I did. But I became more and more frustrated, sitting at home and not making use of my education. So we got a divorce and I moved to Stockholm. What were my chances of getting a good job? Well, I'd heard that one government agency was recruiting a lot of people just then, and it was easy to get in with them, so that's what I tried for and that's what I got. Now, of course, I've got stuck here, but I'd managed to find a job quickly in an emergency when I had to get my life together. Of course, in a way I've spoilt my chances of a real career, but that doesn't bother me too much. I'm no career woman.'

SANDRA, 42, *Law Degree*

When I examined the men's reasons for applying for a particular job, or more often for a job with a particular company, I found strategies of quite a different kind, purposeful and well planned. Some men who failed at the first attempt to get the job they wanted, perhaps in a particular company, would take another but keep in touch with their first choice. A few years later, with more experience and practical knowledge behind them, they would succeed in getting the job they had wanted from the start.

'I wanted to join company X. I'd gathered from friends and acquaintances that I'd be able to get on there. But at the time I qualified, they weren't interested in me—they were mainly looking for computer people and technologists just then. So I thought, "Right, I'll get a job in a computer firm for a few years, and then perhaps I can try again later", and that's what I did about ten years ago. Now I've got as far as I can in Sweden; the next step will be to work in a subsidiary abroad, and then if I do all right, that'll get me a bit further in a few years' time.'

GUNNAR, 45, *MA*

Naturally, there are some women who plan their careers systematically, just as some men find themselves in a particular position or company more or less by chance. However, generally speaking, men have a more purposeful approach. It is also typical that when a woman is asked to describe her job she seems to see it as a series of different tasks to be done. Men, on the other hand, systematically take a more overall view of their positions.

One woman, for example, describes her work in a personnel department as follows:

'I've been working in this office for five years. I'm quite happy with what I have to do, which consists of recruiting staff for overseas posts and advising the training department about the type of courses these people need for their jobs overseas. I assess the situation together with the person concerned, and we work it all out together. One of the nicest things I do is to interview external recruits. Then I really feel I'm using my ability to assess people, and my intuition. When I've done a good recruiting job, I feel pleased.'

A male colleague in the same department describes his job as follows:

'This office hasn't perhaps got very high status and doesn't carry a lot of weight in the company. I really can't say that our work gets much attention, unless we've made some ghastly mistake, which does sometimes happen.
There are selectors responsible for seeing that the right people are chosen for the overseas jobs. I'm a kind of group supervisor, trying to strike a balance between management and unions, and distributing the work among the other selectors as best I can. I have managerial responsibility, but really only for four people. I would like to have more responsibility, and I'd be happy if management recognized the real importance of our work here. But it's the usual thing to look down on personnel work. In the long run—when a suitable opportunity arises—I shall try to apply for something else.'

Thus, if you put the same question about the constituents of the job to a man and a woman, the woman will almost always give a list of ingredients or tasks to be performed while the man will provide a more comprehensive description of the function, and nearly always a further description of the way his job or his function fits into a wider context. This seems to suggest that men take a more global view of their positions and that they are more aware of status and power, and is something to which I will return.

2.5 CAREER IN SLOW MOTION

Many women are probably satisfied with relatively unqualified part-time jobs but those I interviewed were women who were just as eager for promotion as their male counterparts. Only a few had succeeded, however, and then only at a greater cost in effort and time than that expended by men in the same circumstances. The possibility of maternity leave is obviously an important factor here. On an average it takes the childless woman three to four years longer to climb a step up the ladder than her male colleague. For any woman who has been away on maternity leave we would generally have to add a further average delay of two or three years for every pregnancy. I repeat that these are, of course, average figures, but it is quite clear that pauses for childbirth held women back by more than the short period actually 'lost' on maternity leave.

I was repeatedly told how difficult it was to 'get in again' after such leave. One woman described how her desk had been removed and her work divided between three other members of the staff, while another explained that from the day she told her boss she was expecting a child she seemed to become invisible: 'And when I returned seven months later, it was suggested I should go to another department to substitute for a woman on maternity leave there, in a job I knew nothing whatsoever about.'

Behind the problems experienced by women in the child-bearing years several factors can be distinguished. Obviously a company does have a problem when one of its staff is away for several months at a time, particularly if that person occupies a key position. However, the problem is especially awkward in small or medium-sized companies. In larger workplaces such as those included in my studies there are actually more opportunities than are ever exploited for making temporary adjustments in the planning and distribution of work. Quite apart from this, though, many women speak of a more nebulous kind of opposition, something that is difficult to pin down but which comes out clearly in what happens while they are away. One male colleague gets an unexpected opportunity, another is sent on an important course, and so on. In the meantime our new mother has to start from the beginning again: 'It was awful to come back and find I'd become more or less superfluous.' These problems are probably an inevitable result of the rivalry that always obtains on the road to promotion. If you are not on the spot to keep an eye on your interests, you fall behind all too easily. Also, when a young woman has a baby people tend to assume that she will have another in a few years' time, and so she is less likely to be included in corporate career planning, particularly if—as is almost always the case—there are plenty of competent male candidates in the offing. Many companies are in fact uncertain how to tackle these matters: if they ask a new female recruit questions of too personal a nature she may feel sexually discriminated against; and yet, without asking such questions it is more difficult for the company to plan her career.

It is quite clear that pauses like this do delay a women's career and may even stop her having a career at all. Several other studies have shown that career pauses also affect women financially.

2.6 WOMEN GET LESS SUPPORT FROM THE BOSS

If we accept the picture presented in Chapter 1 with its emphasis on mentorship and the role of the group in the advancement of the individual then we should also try to find whether there is any difference in the support provided to men and women in the same workplace by colleagues, subordinates and superiors. It is important to note that I am speaking of support as *perceived* by the individual, because if a male manager is asked about the kind of support and encouragement and 'feedback' that he gives to his subordinates the picture he obtains will be completely different from that one produced by the women themselves. Male managers believe without exception that they treat their subordinates fairly, and that to the best of their ability they provide the necessary feedback and support without confidential chat and valuable company gossip that characterizes all-male communication. I fear that the companies and organizations I have studied are no exception in this respect; rather, they testify to a pattern that is very common in most workplaces.

It was also interesting to note that when men and women were asked about support and communications between colleagues at the same level in the hierarchy both sexes replied positively: that kind of support was perceived as good. However, there was still a sex-related difference in that women talked mainly to other women and men to other men.

Many women hold formal education in excessively high regard, assuming that formal competence is enough to ensure advancement. Unfortunately they do not seem to recognize the importance of the informal rules of the game, or the importance of learning from other people and, in particular, from the boss. They realize that communication with the boss does not function very well, but they fail to see the inhibiting effect of this on their own career chances. I shall return to this topic in Chapter 3.

2.7 CAREER MOTIVATION

Since my investigations revealed women to be no less eager for promotion than men (roughly every third woman and every third man wanted it) I felt it would also be interesting to compare their motivation. Women proved more inclined to mention psychological factors such as 'developing myself' and 'exploiting my inner resources'. Men, on the other hand, talked openly of the need for power and status as their prime incentives. Women put salary before status, after which they mentioned social value (working together with other competent people and being able to develop others) as a major spur. Salary came fairly low on the male list, as did the social value of the job or relations with colleagues.

We can interpret this in several ways. Either the women did not dare to acknowledge the power and status they would like to possess or their incentives really do differ from the men's in that they are more individual-orientated. If this is so, it could help to explain why women so rarely succeed in achieving positions of real power. For it they are competing with men who recognize the importance and the mechanisms of power, while themselves nursing a more idealized picture of the way selection is made (for example, women's exaggerated regard for education), then they are only too likely to be eliminated by male rivals.

The results of my in-depth interviews with women and men can be summarized as follows:

(1) Women do not plan their careers or their first positions as single-mindedly as men.

(2) Women who do succeed have had to expend more effort than a man would have needed to, and it has generally taken them longer to achieve their positions, other things being more or less equal.

(3) Support from subordinates and colleagues is much the same for women as for men. However, the support which a woman receives from her boss is much less adequate, since she misses the kind of informal and often confidential communication which her male colleagues enjoy with their bosses.

(4) The incentives that drive women and men to enjoy a suc-

cessful career are probably different. Women are not so ready to talk about careers in terms of status and power. They are more likely to be motivated by psychological factors and a desire for self-realization.

Thus the difficulties facing women may depend, to some extent, on themselves, but the type of leadership and norms which govern the selection of promising managerial candidates also goes a long way towards explaining the situation. In order to broaden the picture and to see whether lack of support from the boss, for example, was the general rule I conducted a series of polls and received answers from several hundred people of both sexes. These investigations will be described in Chapter 3.

Chapter 3

DIFFERENT WORLDS?

To complement the picture that emerged from the interviews reported above I held polls at a number of workplaces. I wanted to see whether men and women differed consistently in their attitude towards sex equality, career opportunities and similar issues. The questions on which the poll was based were designed after talking to groups of women at their workplaces, thus indirectly reflecting the kinds of myths and problems that these women perceived at work and in their environment in general.

The polls as a whole are presented below. They were designed more or less identically in the various organizations and the results are given here in summarized form: the different answers have been combined to produce average figures, since it was found out that the differences between the answers of the two sexes followed virtually the same pattern at the various workplaces.

3.1 EQUAL CAREER AND DEVELOPMENT OPPORTUNITIES?

Seven of the questions concerned career and development opportunities. These are reproduced below, together with an account of the answers.

(1) Are opportunities for part-time work the same for both sexes?

Sixty-five per cent of the women believed the opportunities to be the same; 60 per cent of the men thought so. There is thus no great difference between men and women on this point.

(2) Are maternity and paternity leave equally available?

To this question about 60 per cent of both sexes answered 'yes'.

However, this affirmation probably refers only to what people regard as their legal right. Other studies have shown that cases of paternity leave are, in reality, extremely rare in Sweden, despite legislation which is intended to encourage it. On the other hand, views on the opportunities for training and development within the company clearly diverge.

(3) Are opportunities for training in the organization the same for both sexes?

To this question only 30 per cent of the women answered 'yes', while a little over 70 per cent of the men believe that women enjoy the same opportunities as they do themselves. This discrepancy persisted, albeit slightly less markedly, when people assessed the situation in their own departments.

(4) Are opportunities for training and development in your department the same regardless of sex?

To this question 53 per cent of the women and 74 per cent of the men replied that the opportunities in their department were the same for women and for men. The men also gave much the same response with regard to the company as a whole, while the women were more pessimistic on this point, which might be related to the fact that men obtain more information than women about conditions outside their own departments.

(5) Does promotion occur without reference to sex?

Here again, women and men saw things quite differently: 82 per cent of the men thought this was so, as against only 30 per cent of the women. This divergence is hardly surprising, as women only have to look around them to see that most of their female colleagues have not been promoted.

However, I also wanted to find out how women and men explained this state of affairs to themselves, i.e. that women did not advance to the same extent as men. An open question was therefore included, asking respondents to indicate what they considered to be the three most important reasons for this situation.

(6) Women do not advance in our organization to the same extent as men because...

The women suggested the following reasons as the most important:

(a) That women do not, or cannot, get the kind of training that leads to promotion;
(b) That women start off in jobs which do not lead to promotion;
(c) That the bosses take less notice of women.

The men, on the other hand, believed that women failed to achieve promotion because:

(a) They do not get enough support from their families;
(b) They dare not take risks;
(c) They do not really want promotion.

The *women* thus referred to *factors connected with the job* and with management, while the *men looked for psychological explanations* in the personal situation or mentality of the women. This divergence recurs in the answers to the next question.

(7) Why do men succeed in advancing (at work) to a greater extent than women?

To the women the three most important reasons were that:

(a) Men have an eye to their careers from the first time they get a job;
(b) Men get more support and encouragement from their bosses;
(c) It is easier for men to get further training.

The men, on the other hand, saw the following as the three most important reasons why women are inclined to fall behind:

(a) Men get more support and encouragement from their families;
(b) Men have more self-confidence;
(c) Men expect more.

Once again, the women referred to reasons connected with personnel policy (support of boss, training, etc.) while the men mentioned only personal, psychological and private factors: support from the family, self-confidence, demands. *In other words, they spoke of just those personal factors which they thought the women lacked.*

It seems obvious that if bosses in general, and the men responsible for personnel matters, cherish their own idea of what *they* believe is stopping women, and that this is quite different from the picture suggested by the answers of the women themselves, then it is certainly going to be difficult to promote measures likely to support equality. The tendency to dismiss women's 'difficulties' by invoking psychological arguments can also be found in much American research from the early 1970s (see, for example, Burrow, 1978). It was not until researchers versed in organizational theory and sociology (such as Rosabeth Moss-Kanter) began to study the implications of organizational structure and leadership for women's promotion opportunities (Moss-Kanter, 1977) that we really acquired a new perspective on the common psychological myths that women 'do not want', 'do not dare', 'are not able' and so on.

Up to now we have been looking at how men and women develop opportunities in the company in general terms. Let us now examine whether the sex-related differences in the answers still hold when we ask people instead about their *own personal* opportunities.

On the question of further training there do not seem to be any great differences in what men and women regard as possible: usually they regard the formal opportunities for further training as equal. In practice, however, it is the men who take part in the longer and more management training and residential courses. Furthermore, women are more likely to go on courses outside the company and in their own time, often explaining that they want 'a bit of paper to show for it'. Thus a woman is prepared to go to evening classes, perhaps in business administration at a polytechnic or university, while a man acquires the same type of knowledge at a residential course or by self-tuition. Perhaps this difference is also related to that exaggerated faith in education and formal competence which I have already mentioned as a common feature in women.

Another set of answers which—perhaps unexpectedly—shows no sex-related divergence concerns the desire for promotion, the will to take up a more responsible post. Sixty per cent of the women and 60 per cent of the men declared their readiness to assume such responsibility. However, when assessing the actual likelihood of the opportunity arising, only 8 per cent of the women felt that they had a reasonable chance, while as many as 70 per cent of the men assumed that their own chances were very good. Whether this testifies to women's realism and to men's 'I- can't-see-any-obstacle' attitude, I shall not attempt to say; but it does not seem unlikely that the difference in attitude has its effect on the outcome: there may well be a negative self-reinforcing effect, whereby people who do not believe in the existence of promotion opportunities for themselves do not in fact get promoted.

3.2 ATTITUDES TO SEX-DISCRIMINATION POLICIES

In answer to the question 'Are you familiar with the sex-discrimination laws?' almost twice as many men as women answered 'Yes, reasonably'. However, it appears that women were slightly more positive about the laws than men (though perhaps not as much more as one might expect): 34 per cent of the women studied were definitely positive as against 20 per cent of the men.

Although men and women have much the same opinions about the laws as such, there is a striking difference when assessing whether it would be difficult to promote greater equality in their own companies. Sixty-five per cent of the men thought it would be easy while only 20 per cent of the women agreed with them.

An increase in part-time managerial positions is often mentioned in the sex-discrimination debate as a way of achieving greater equality. Here the views of the two sexes diverge: only 30 per cent of the men felt positive about a change of this kind while as many as 70 per cent of the women were in favour. Thus we can conclude that, in general, men and women feel equally favourable towards the sex-discrimination laws, but women envisage considerable problems when working for more equality in their own companies.

Various ways of achieving greater equality are also viewed differently by men and women. Both sexes would like to see more women in male-dominated occupations, but only women also want to see more men in female-dominated jobs.

In one of the companies studied we also asked a few rather general attitude-probing questions, but the answers did not yield as much information about sex-related differences as we had expected. Nevertheless, as part of our picture of the 'different worlds', they can perhaps give us some idea of the preconceived ideas that actually prevail.

(1) 'A male manager has a wider contact network.'

Both men and women (a few more women) believe that male managers generally enjoy a wider contact network.

(2) 'Career women are often selfish.'

Seventy-nine per cent of the men and 73 per cent of the women *disagreed* with this statement.

(3) 'Men support one another.'

Here views diverge. Seventy per cent of the women claim that 'men do support one another' while 60 per cent of the men deny that this is so.

(4) 'Career women are unfeminine.'

Both men (82 per cent) and women (98 per cent) disagree with this statement.

(5) 'Men should accept equal responsibility for home and family.'

The replies are quite clear on this point: both men and women agree with the statement.

(6) 'Women can't help one another as men do.'

This statement is, of course, a mirror image of the one about men supporting one another, and, as we would expect, the responses reveal diverging views. Sixty-seven per cent of the men believe that women can help one another while only 36 per cent of the women agree.

(7) 'Men cannot take on equal responsibility for home and family.'

Women and men agree on this point. Sixty-five per cent of the men and 62 per cent of the women feel that a man cannot take on the same responsibility for home and family as a woman.

(8) 'Men managers prefer to work with men.'

Eighty-three per cent of the women believe that men prefer to work with other men but only 45 per cent of the men agree with them.

(9) 'Women are better suited to looking after children.'

Thirty-two per cent of the women and 53 per cent of the men believe that women are more suited to looking after children. We have already found both sexes agreeing that men should but cannot assume equal responsibility for home and family (over 60 per cent agreed on this). Nevertheless, when we tighten up the question and ask whether women are better suited to the task, we find more men believing that women are better suited to looking after children.

(10) 'Men are afraid of clever women.'

On this point opinions differ greatly: 70 per cent of the men denied the truth of the statement while as many as 85 per cent of the women agree that men are afraid of clever women.

(11) 'A woman who wants to get on generally has to be that bit better than her male colleagues.'

Men and women both agree with this statement: 71 per cent of the men and 81 per cent of the women.

(12) 'Women bosses are often more strict than men.'

Here the two sexes thought much the same: only 16 per cent of the men and 28 per cent of the women agreed with the statement.

(13) 'A woman manager can never get top management to listen to her views as they would listen to a man in a similar position.'

Both sexes (women 64 per cent, men 65 per cent) agreed that a woman manager finds it more difficult to get a hearing for her views than a man in a similar position.

(14) 'Women with children should not pursue a career.'

Here views were largely the same: 66 per cent of the men and 56 per cent of the women felt that women with families should not pursue a career.

(15) 'Women show less initiative than men.'

Here men and women agree: 86 per cent of the men and 93 per cent of the women deny that women show less initiative than men.

The following are the most important conclusions suggested by this attitude study:

(1) Women believe that 'men support one another' but men disagree with their view.
(2) Women do not believe that women can help one another; men believe they can.
(3) Women believe that men prefer to work with other men, but most men deny this.
(4) Women believe that men are afraid of clever women, but men disagree.

On all these points the two sexes clearly disagree, but it is also interesting to note the topics on which they do agree:

(1) A male manager has a wider contact network.
(2) A woman pursuing a career needs be neither selfish nor unfeminine.
(3) A man should, but cannot, assume equal responsibility for home and family, but women are better suited to the responsibilities of the home, more than half agree that a woman with children should not pursue a career.
(4) A woman who wants to pursue a career often has to be better at it than a male colleague.

(5) A woman manager is not more strict than her male coun-
    terpart.

(6) A woman manager cannot persuade senior management to
    give her the same hearing for her views that they would
    give to a man.

Women and men have different approaches to work. From the
beginning, men appear to be more goal-orientated, thinking in
terms of careers. Women seem to look at their work in a more
limited way, evaluating it chiefly for its content (the actual tasks
involved). Women who want to get on, and who have done so, are
wary of speaking of career needs, power or status. They prefer to
emphasize self-realization, and set more store by human interactions at work than 'career men'. These points were discussed in
Chapter 2.

When we turn to attitudes to career opportunities, further education and promotion as actually achieved we are surely justified
in claiming the existence of two cultures within the workplace:
one woman's world and one man's. Women are more pessimistic
than men in assessing their own chances and opportunities. If we
look at the hierarchial order of things as it is today we have to
admit that the women's view is also the more realistic. Yet men
seem to persist in believing that opportunities are equal and that
women 'have only themselves to blame' if they fail to get on,
as their failure depends on psychological factors. Since men also
set a psychological emphasis on their own advancement, claiming
that it is self-confidence and personal (emotional?) support from
the family that encourages success, it seems clear that 'it depends
on the individual' is a very strongly held conviction. However,
women are less convinced of this. If a male boss can 'blame' a
woman's failure to advance on the fact that she does not really
want promotion, or that her lack of self-confidence stems from
family circumstances, he is simply providing his conscience with

a ready-made alibi. Naturally, by no means all men think in this way, but the interesting aspect about a broad based poll of the kind I have described is that it provides a good general survey of prevalent attitudes.

The differences in the men's and women's answers are too obvious to be easily explained away, and so long as people dare not even look to see whether such differences exist in their own workplaces we cannot hope for change.

The men's world is, of course, the bosses' world, since the bosses are almost exclusively men. Also it is fairly obvious that the general agreement on attitudes and values in this male world is underpinned by the much more intensive and frequent communication that men enjoy with one another—be it between colleagues at the same level or between the boss and his subordinates. It is easier and more natural to communicate with someone resembling oneself, and so male bosses function better in their relations with other men. This argument will be developed in Chapter 4.

Chapter 4

ON MEN'S TERMS

4.1 WHAT IS AN ORGANIZATIONAL CULTURE?

'But I don't want a career on *men's terms!*'—this is the cry from the heart that many women will recognize as their own, and I have often noticed that we women 'understand' intuitively what we mean by 'on men's terms'. At least, we seldom trouble to explain the words, using them rather as a kind of secret code. In this chapter I shall describe what I consider to be 'men's terms', and I shall suggest that a whole range of organizational norms and game rules are embraced by these three words.

Every organization has a culture peculiar to itself, which any skilled consultant will readily recognize, probably experiencing it as a characteristic spirit or climate that pervades the company, sometimes positive and open, sometimes negative and closed.

If, as we assume, every organizational culture is moulded and governed by certain norms and values then it will be necessary to distinguish between openly stated or *explicit* norms and unstated or *implicit* ones before we can assess the climate of a particular organization. In a healthy, open and creative organizational culture there will be very little discrepancy between explicit and implicit norms; the people in such a climate live as they teach.

In a poor organizational culture, on the other hand, the stated and unstated norms are often in conflict. For instance, management may proclaim its interest in encouraging creativity and initiative but simultaneously an unstated norm may imply that no-one should question what the bosses decide. Official personnel policy may express a wish to support self-development and improvement along employees, whereas company practice may fall far short of this ideal. In such cases the employees receive contradictory signals; they see that the expressed goals are not being realized, but any mention of the fact would be taboo. In this kind of environment people become passive, frightened and inefficient.

They cannot promote efficiency, either their own or that of the organization.

What can be done to change a poor organizational culture? Can we even envisage breaking this type of negative behaviour pattern without changing the whole culture? As an organizational consultant these are the questions with which I have been battling for many years, and I am still reasonably optimistic that it is possible to change a culture, although I am slightly less so about the possibility of influencing those basic norms apparently based on what women call 'men's terms'. Whether a culture is defined as good or bad, men's norms are always paramount at those levels in the hierarchy where real freedom to make decisions occurs. At lower levels, where people are busy with fairly routine autonomous tasks, it is possible to create a limited subculture. However, this can never be more than an insignificant separate world, at least so long as it does satisfactorily whatever it is supposed to do. Examples of such submerged female cultures which are largely left to lead their own lives are not hard to find: cleaners, night nurses, packers, office girls and so on. They all believe their own work is an important part of the whole; but in fact it is a very small cog in a very large wheel on which members of the subculture have very little influence. Therefore their culture flourishes in a world of its own, far from the centres of power and influence.

4.2 MALE NORMS IN THE DECISION-MAKING CULTURE

Male norms have obviously steered (and still steer) the culture which pervades the decision-making world, i.e. the top strata in the many hierarchies around us. By 'obviously' I simply mean in this context that in the past the most senior positions have been occupied by men, and they still are. No-one should thus find it strange that the prevailing norms have always been and are still being applied by men. That this is so 'obvious' may or may not be a good thing in a broader human perspective, of course, but that is another matter.

However, it is not a good thing, and I base this conclusion largely on what we seem to have achieved to date. In many respects we still have a long way to go, and our modern world still has many unsolved and, in human terms, difficult problems to face. It cannot be called a good world when half the global population suffers empty bellies and starved minds, and many people are unable even to write their names or to enjoy a reasonable chance of testing their own potential. It cannot be called a good world, when people enslave and kill one another out of ignorance and fear. It cannot be called a good world in which we have built stocks of devastating weapons without any proper control—they are not to be used, but they are there. It would be easy to blame all this on men and their blind love of effective action, as do many feminists and pacifists. However, in this I am unwilling to concur, but I do believe that *everyone*—men and women alike—must acknowledge the problems and try to tackle them in new ways, calling for personal strength and the courage to question and challenge old norms. This will be possible one day, but it will take a long time and a lot of energy, as the traditions and norms of centuries cannot be expected to change overnight.

What are these inherited masculine norms? How strong are they and what impact do they have on the organizational cultures of today? The hierarchy, as a structure, is the setting in which the norms operate, and at this point we should perhaps stop and ask ourselves why this particular structure has for so long surpassed any other as a vehicle for the efficient production of goods and services. Military systems have always been hierarchical, and so have religious institutions—both of them the tools of their respective ideologies. They have operated with extreme efficiency, through their harsh and unequivocal demands on the loyalty of their members at all levels in the hierarchy. The priest leads the congregation, but above him is the bishop, above the bishop, the archbishop and so on up to the highest authority of all, be it God, Allah, or some other supreme being whose role is undisputed. Down through the hierarchy the message of the supreme ruler passes, more or less unaltered. The paramount rule has always been that if calls for change become *too* radical among the lower ranks, then the offending member (or members) is replaced by another more obedient and loyal. The superior structural qualities of the hierarchy (as a model) appear to emerge from its ability—at least so long as it continues to avert chaos and hold revolution in check—to capture and exploit biological natural selection.

Let us assume that the Supreme Deity's chief representative on Earth is a man who clearly possesses the intelligence and the personal qualities needed to keep the rest of the flock in their places, and that he manages to find disciples to cope effectively with all the problems right down the line, so that the words and laws of the Deity operate at every level. If all this holds good, then we have a truly effective chain of command. However, as is widely recognized, the ability to choose the right team is one of the most important attributes of the successful business leader, and one that by no means always work to perfection. After all, the leader not only has to be a good judge of the essential attributes such as intelligence, social skills and strength but he also has to be able to discern those often indefinable qualities that are linked to change and renewal. This is just where the difficulty lies: these last qualities are not always encouraged or even accepted in the traditional effective hierarchy; in fact they are far more likely to develop among people in a free environment, on the periphery or borderlands of the established hierarchical apparatus. Thus people possessing these innovative qualities are not usually part of the establishment, and established leaders are more or less blind to the kind of contribution they could make.

Thus while *elitism* is the essential norm on which the supremacy of the hierarchy as an organizational form is based it is also the weakest part of its foundations, because if elitism fails to operate satisfactorily, then people inside and even outside the hierarchy will not only openly oppose the structure itself but will also protest against the message that it transmits.

Elitism as a norm is closely linked to the idea of *competition*, and to the belief that competition exists and that it works well. Of course, 'competition' can mean many different things, but for our present purpose we can define it by a simple illustration. If we have to choose between *two* people, then let them show us what they can do and we will choose the best! In other words, the two compete according to certain approved or at least acknowledged rules, and we expect that one of them will win (justice is guaranteed by the rules); the relative skill of the two competitors in whatever qualities are being tested will determine the outcome. The male-dominated tradition in sports is based exclusively on this principle.

Elitism, and the competition that it implies, goes back to an age-old male norm system, well characterized by the Spartan attitude to trials of strength and competitive games in ancient Greece. Since early times men have competed against one another, in a setting where physical and psychological endurance are the supreme qualities. In order to learn to bear physical and mental pain, men also have to learn to suppress other, softer qualities— emotionality, playfulness and tenderness.

Of the two halves of the human brain, the left is said to be linked to analytical ability and rationality while the right has a more emotional and holistic orientation. It has also been suggested by some scientists that in men (but not in women) the left hemisphere has developed more strongly in comparison with the right. I am not one to delight in dividing men and women into two camps, or in dividing the brain into halves which are then neatly matched with one or other of the two groups. Such theories are all too simple, although they can trigger off some stimulating arguments and suggest some fruitful ideas. One such idea, which was suggested to me by personal experience, is that the traditional sex roles with their inhibiting impact on human potential, may well have meant that girls and women are rewarded for developing certain qualities of the right hemisphere such as caring, feeling and creativity in a broad sense while men and boys are rewarded—not least by the opposite sex—for developing qualities linked with the left half of the brain, such as analytical capacity and rationality.

Having said that, nonetheless it seems that the norms we are discussing here cannot be explained in a single dimension, for instance in terms of traditional sex roles and socialization. In the men who apply them they have certainly come to include many of the qualities attaching to the left half of the brain. However, this really only means that the norms are even more intractable than if they simply sprang from tradition and upbringing, since there may be fundamental genetic differences also explaining why men more readily develop the qualities of the left half of the brain.

Whether such genetic differences actually exist is still open to question, and is anyway not particularly relevant to my present argument. On the other hand, it is interesting to note recent research in the United States which suggests that androgynous individuals (and leaders) are simultaneously achievement-orientated and emotion-orientated, and that differences in the behaviour of effective leaders are not sex-dependent (Humphrey and Schrode, 1978).

Returning for a moment to the Spartans' world I have described above, I would suggest that although this contains a strong element of elitism as manifested in endurance and the suppression of feelings it also includes a large amount of emotionalism, though not, of course, expressed in blushes or tears.

It does not seem possible that any man or boy could survive in a world where everything depends on winning but where everyone sometimes loses (there is a limit to everyone's skill and capacity) unless he also enjoyed some sense of community and belonging. In fact this feeling is extremely important to him, since it provides the reward and/or the compensation for the effort he is prepared to make. That he is forced to make an effort, to give of himself, is clear. It is part of the system that the competition should require the maximum sacrifice of its participants.

Returning now to the world of the decision-makers, we find that the rules of their system are quite explicit. Even the language with which they describe their situation and the sacrifices which they make shows exactly what is at stake. No reader will fail to recognize the man who exclaims: 'Of course my family suffers!' or the two men holding the following conversation:

A: (an older manager): Are you at home next week?
B: (a younger colleague): No, I'm at work as usual.
A: Well, of course, that's what I meant.

'Home' is his job. His family is his 'other life' which often has to 'suffer', which has no natural part in the competitive game that fills his time.

In concrete terms it is possible to reckon just how many hours male decision-makers can spare for their private lives. On average, they work for 12–13 of their waking hours, sleep for 7–8, while 3–4 hours are 'left' for other things. This applies not only to those at the top of the hierarchy.

In arguments about the pros and cons of day nurseries for children it is often pointed out that the quality rather than the quantity of the time parents spend with their children is what determines the success of the relationship, and the same argument is often invoked with respect to the decision-maker's family life. However, we have to remember that a child attends day nursery for a few years only at the beginning of its life, whereas the striving decision-maker may devote 30–40 years of his life to his career: 30–40 years during which he is more or less compelled to find his emotional rewards in the setting where he spends so much time, which naturally enough, means establishing strong emotional ties with the other people there. These ties are ultimately regularized in the mentorship system and in professional solidarity—positive arrangements in themselves if only they did not also so often lead to sectarianism and isolationism.

This kind of sectarianism can assume many forms, from the business leader who surrounds himself with a few men of similar bent and roughly his own age, a model which we could call the 'gang model', to the more traditional 'buddies model', in which two people complement each other in various ways so that together they represent a powerful constellation, and the 'football coach model' in which a strong leader surrounds himself with a set of selected young hopefuls.

The team spirit, and the loyalty and emotional ties which blossom in these teams, are often reinforced by the possession of a common educational background and other experiences. In Sweden many industrial leaders have trained as engineers and/or economists; in many countries they may have belonged to the same fraternity, have gone to the same school, have become members of the same clubs, or have been in the same regiment. As a result, they find it easy to understand each other's language and to share one another's values. In view of all this, do women really have much change of breaking into the team? What can they contribute? What would they be forced to sacrifice in order to be accepted on men's terms?

4.3 CAN WOMEN COMPETE ON MEN'S TERMS?

That many women feel unwilling to compete on men's terms is one thing. Whether it is in fact feasible to combine this competition with a reasonably normal woman's life is quite another. Whether the male bosses actually give those women prepared 'to do the impossible' a chance is another thing again.

That women fail to reach the really senior positions in large corporations is hardly surprising: a 12–14-hour working day, very little time off, and innumerable long and tiring journeys all call for a sacrifice of private life which many women are not prepared to make, at least until their children have grown up. However, even childless women probably find it almost as difficult to devote themselves so whole-heartedly to their professional role, barring a few obvious exceptions, particularly in the United States.

However, what about the jobs just below this level, belonging to what is sometimes called higher middle management, that perhaps do not call for quite so much commitment and devotion? In fact, these jobs are still quite demanding, for two reasons. First, at these levels there is almost continual rivalry for promotion to the next step above. Although everyone recognizes that few, if any, will achieve this, people are nonetheless spurred by the possibility, and the competition and rivalry is correspondingly harsh. The second factor is one which applies particularly to women: paradoxically, perhaps it is also at just this level that the (male) gang is most in evidence, with the strong sense of community we have discussed before, and so it is not particularly surprising to find men introducing one another into the team at this point.

However, it is at the next level down (middle management) that we find most women managers today, but they are generally older than their male colleagues (see our earlier discussion of the time it takes for women to gain promotion), and, given contemporary career-planning cycles, this makes any idea of further promotion most unlikely for them.

In Sweden, and no doubt in other European countries, an informal rule is applied whereby further training is not provided for people over 35. This is naturally very unfavourable to women. It seems that the relative success of American women in obtaining managerial positions is partly due to the greater frequency in the American companies of in-house schemes. In addition, any woman who unexpectedly persists beyond the middle-management level, trying to compete for a higher post, will have to be prepared to face much unpleasant attention.

While being forced to agree that her own weakness, and her lack of perseverence and aggressiveness, is probably what checks her at this stage, we must also recognize the excessive problems she would have had to overcome. In extensive research on discrimination Moss-Kanter (1977) has revealed discrimination factors that affect many different kinds of minority, and there is no doubt that a single female in an otherwise male group of managers will certainly come up against most of them. Drawing on Moss-Kanter's theories I shall briefly summarize some of these problems below.

4.4 HOW IS THE 'ODD' WOMAN MANAGER TREATED?

The fact that you are a single example of your kind in a group, that you represent a minority of one, inevitably makes you the subject of extra attention. Let us call this the 'spotlight effect'. There are, of course, certain positive aspects: you will certainly be seen and heard. There are always negative aspects as well: no mistakes can be made; any that do occur will be magnified and may lead to *stereotyping*. In other words, people tend to expect that a mistake or a kind of behaviour will be repeated, that it is 'typical'. Many myths about women managers have developed in this way. For example:

(1) A woman manager is often forced to be tougher and harder than a man in order to gain respect.
(2) A woman is always better prepared when she comes to a meeting.
(3) A woman manager is much more understanding and better at listening than a man would be.

These last two statements are admittedly positive, but, like all stereotyped expectations, they still divert attention from the individual herself, categorizing her and tethering her to a role which she has to live up to, even if, as an *individual*, she does not fit into it. If she is not particularly good at listening to people she will be adjudged 'unfeminine'. Unfortunately, men are not the only ones to support this stereotype; women do it as well, perhaps particularly those who have not tried the difficult and lonely role of the leader.

Since it is not acceptable to make a few mistakes and since, on the contrary, such mistakes will be exaggerated in the telling, the woman manager who wants to develop herself and who is courageous enough to learn will be under a terrible strain. Learning always calls for a certain amount of experimentation; the learner must be allowed the option of sometimes making mistakes.

Another oppressive effect of stereotyping is that any women manager becomes a model, a kind of representative or spokesperson, for all other women. This may be something quite foreign to her own wishes, but it is an inevitable result of her being the 'only one'. I have often been in this situation myself (for instance, as the only women on an all-male teachers' council) and I have found myself watching my words with extreme caution, knowing that everything I say will be carefully scrutinized and may set a norm for a long time to come.

Thus being a woman manager almost always subjects you to assessment in many more ways than your male colleagues are exposed to, and, what is probably hardest to bear, you have no little gang of your own to give you the necessary courage and comfort. There is an unavoidable element of loneliness in all leadership roles, but for a woman it has extra dimensions that a man is spared.

4.5 CAN THE 'MEN'S TERMS' BE ALTERED?

The main topic of this chapter concerns the difficulties which confront people, particularly women, when they attain a position of leadership at the top of the hierarchy. I have also pointed out that the traditional hierarchical system has so far proved effective in the mass production of goods and services. The question is thus whether we can envisage other organizational forms and other cultures in which women and even men could function 'better' in their managerial roles: 'better' in the sense of more easily combining private and professional roles; of men and women competing on equal terms; of efficiently achieving the goals of the organization through the efforts of individuals permitted to develop and realize their whole personalities. I shall be discussing these questions in Chapters 5 and 6. For the moment I will only say that I believe such organizational systems *are* possible and that we can envisage a 'new' managerial role for the future.

I would even go further: if we do not create organizational cultures of this kind, then our future will be a dark one. If we fail to exploit all the human resources we possess, how can we believe in a dignified future for our daughters and our sons?

Chapter 5

TWO-CAREER FAMILIES AND NEW LIFE PATTERNS

5.1 TWO JOBS OR TWO CAREERS?

1 pkt margarine
2 pints milk
1 yoghourt
12 eggs
Cheese—you know the sort
Parsley
Tomatoes
Fish fingers
Grapes
Loo paper
Conditioner
Ice-cream
Flowers (yellow or pink)
A bit of smoked salmon, if you think it's OK.

This is a modern *billet doux*. I have lost count of the times I have written notes like this to my husband. In another age he might have written home to me:

'Darling,
I've arrived in London. I'm thinking about you and the children. Trips like this aren't as much fun as you think. I miss you, and I hate sleeping alone ...'

However, in a two-career family any letters we manage to write to one another are nearly always geared to ideas which have to be transformed into action if the everyday business of our joint lives is to work at all.

Let us look at another episode in the life of the two-career family. It is the school holidays, and the mother and father have taken the two children with them on a business trip to New York.

The family books in at a suitable hotel. They have organized everything down to the last detail. 'We'll take it in turns to go to meetings. You can have Monday and half Tuesday; on a Wednesday I'll be flying to Boston, you'll have to take the children ...' Then something occurs which has not been allowed for, but which in fact often happens around Easter in New York: there is a snowstorm. Chaos, traffic jams, taxis stuck, cancelled flights—it is hardly possible to get out of the door. All meetings are cancelled, no-one can get to them on Manhattan, and it is even more difficult for them to get out. Everything has to be dealt with by telephone—the only system that still works. The mother and father in the two-career family then go into action as follows:

(1) Take the elevator to the drugstore in the hotel. Buy foam bath oil, body paints, and funny little animals which can swim when you wind them up.

(2) Fill the bath with plenty of warm water and let the children loose in an orgy of water games. In the meantime she makes her business calls from the room while he goes down to the lobby to do his. When the children have been splashing for two hours, they have had enough. Adults and children then swap 'offices'. The children get the bedroom and the television, the parents use the telephone extension in the bathroom and continue working. A two-career family, particularly if the children are allowed to take an active part in their parents' lives, must always plan for crises and be prepared to improvise.

Another typical episode in a two-career life pattern would be as follows:

'Darling, I know you've got to prepare your notes for tomorrow's lecture, but you know I've got to get mine ready as well

... And don't forget, it's the same conference we're going to!'

But who is to put the children to bed? If families can cope with conflicts like this there is a chance for them to live an exciting and different kind of life.

However, what exactly is meant by the two-career family or the dual-career couple? It certainly implies more than a relationship in which both partners are working. Hall and Hall (1979), who have written several books about dual careers, make the following distinction:

> A couple in which both partners work outside the home may be referred to as a dual-job couple, but if the work is important for personal development as well as for the household income—then we may say that they are a dual-career couple. Dual-career couples are also defined by life-style, a life-style designed to support, encourage and facilitate—not just to tolerate—the career pursuits of both members.

In other words, it is largely the life-style that determines whether we are talking about a dual-career family or about a family in which both partners happen to have jobs. I would even go so far as to include possible children in the life pattern of the dual-career family. Since both parents have to plan and utilize their lives and their leisure in a special way they must also consider their children in a way that is different from the pattern in the more traditional set-up. By 'consider' I mean that the children are often involved in different parts of their parent's lives, and that, when necessary, either if both parents can look after them independently.

The idea of the dual-career family thus seems to embrace a whole new life-style which has evolved as both partners strive to pursue independent professional careers while also supporting one another as far as possible. However, one may well wonder whether the earlier model of the 'businessman and the housewife' was not also a dual-career family in its way. It was undeniably a 'two-job family', and perhaps a lot more than that.

All those women who for years provide the back-up service and bring up the children unaided, who sacrifice much of their own time to business entertaining—are they not playing an important part in promoting their husbands' careers? Certainly they are, but unfortunately their contribution is entirely dependent on their husband's success, and the social and economic rewards are his. Of course, there are also rewards for the woman, perhaps exciting trips or an entertaining life and interesting social contacts, but she has little opportunity for self-realization outside her family life. The partners in such a relationship have 'specialized' their lives: one has become 'expert' on the private aspects of life and the other on the professional. A woman who holds power exclusively in relation to her partner's standing, and who in turn 'owns' the private functions attaching to the relationship, will often put an excessive amount of effort into defending her territory. Understandably, but unfortunately, some even seek consciously to exclude their partners from their children's lives and development. Among those who suffer from this we often find the woman herself: the children grow up and make their own lives, taking with them much of their mother's source of power. Their father, denied an active role in his children's development, misses one of life's most valuable experiences. In a modern two-career family the balance of power between partners is a more complex affair: neither of them 'owns' the children, nor do they 'own' one another. Instead, both partners are economically and socially independent, and their relationship must therefore be the result of real feelings and voluntary decisions.

How widespread is the new dual-career life-style? In the United States the number of two-career families is said to have been increasing throughout the 1970s (Rice, 1979), and today there are probably between 3 and 4 million such families in that country. In the past it was often a question of 'marrying the girl next door', but today when women and men meet not only at the local dance hall but often also far from home as they attend conferences or courses or find themselves in other 'interesting' setting, then personal choice can be based on a wider range of criteria than when it is restricted (metaphorically) to the house next door. It is therefore not surprising that young people with the same kind of interests or goals in life (and thus probably with the same high level of education) decide to join their lives, although the focus of their education and the fields they have chosen to work in may be quite different.

No research has been done on this subject in Sweden, but I would imagine the trend to be much the same as in the United States, which point in rather different directions. On the one hand, it is becoming increasingly common for career women to marry and have children (Henning and Jardin, 1977), while on the other, divorce is becoming more frequent among women pursuing careers. Formerly the proportion of 'singles' was greater among women managers than among women in general (or among male managers), and women managers also had fewer children than average (Fogarty *et al.*, 1971). Now, as we can see, this trend has been broken, and a new generation of career women between the ages of 30 and 45 is emerging, just as likely to have families but more liable to divorce than the 'average woman'. This can—and often is—explained in terms of the greater stress imposed on women who have become more anxious to combine a full life as a woman with a self-developing one as a professional person, something which, in fact, is just as difficult to realize as it ever was.

However, in my interviews with women managers I have often noticed that the reasons for divorce are not always as self-evident as the American studies would suggest. Many women mentioned other reasons for the breakdown of their marriages, apart from stress and the practical difficulties involved in satisfying different role expectations. As they saw it, they had simply grown away from their partners and 'developed themselves out of the relationship'. However. it seems likely that this personal development would not have progressed as fast, or even perhaps have started at all, if the women concerned had not regarded a career as an important goal in life with a value of its own. So perhaps, after all, the family situation has been impaired in some way by the wife's professional or career ambitions,. In Sweden, for example, no research has been carried out which could tell us whether the divorce rate is higher in two-career families than it is in a cross-section of the population as a whole—something which might also tell us whether (and how) the new life-style may ultimately change our society.

As my interviews with women managers about the way they live their lives are not based on any large or systematically selected samples, my illustrations in the following section must be taken as a pointer towards an eventual formulation of some more precise questions or hypotheses rather than as the results of scientific research.

5.2 THE DIFFERENT ROLES OF THE WOMAN MANAGER

'To start with, you see, my job called for a lot of long trips even when the children were small, so Bob had to be mainly responsible for the family while I was away. Everything was fine at first, but gradually I noticed that Bob was asking more and more of me when I was at home. I just couldn't get him to understand how tired and wound up I was, after two week's buying in Singapore, for instance. I needed a couple of days to catch up with myself and all the things to do at home, but Bob expected me to be able to change gear straight away. He might have arranged a family party or invited some neighbours in the day after my return, and then if I was annoyed I was told that the least I could do was to join in things now I was at home. Life hadn't been much fun for him recently, and so on and so on. That's how our ridiculous quarrels began. I thought he could make a bit of an effort—after all, it was only going to be for a few years. Once I'd been promoted I wouldn't have to travel so much. But he couldn't accept that; he simply said that later was later, and the children would be older then anyway, and why couldn't I be like other women who wanted to be with their families and so on. I began to see him in a new light. It suddenly struck me that he didn't seem to have any ambition to get on, to make something of himself, and all this made me start thinking about divorce. I was still fond of Bob at a certain level, but we were slipping further and further away from one another.'

INGRID, 42, *Head Buyer*

'I'll tell you what's most difficult about my life at the moment. It's not having enough time, not having enough time to visit my parents although I know they're not getting any younger, not having time to meet any friends except those at work, not having time to hit a golf ball the whole season although I'd promised myself last year that I would, never having time to go to the children's school, never having time ... never having time to live!'

CHRISTINA, 39

Both these women have children, and it seems fairly obvious that much of their stress and their sense of never having enough time springs from their maternal role. However, let us consider for a moment some of the many roles and relationships that a professional career woman may have to fulfil simultaneously. Table 5.1 includes a selection of these, and they are all roles which make heavy and sometimes incompatible demands on the individual woman's emotional and intellectual resources.

Table 5.1   Some common roles for a woman

Role	
	Own children
Mother	
	Partner's children
Wife/partner/mistress	
Daughter	
Sister	
Friend	
Colleague	
Boss	

To be a mother to one's own children, and possibly also to those of a partner, is always a demanding business, and is no less so for the mother in a dual-career family. Being 'mother' in a family even when it is possible to share most of the practical responsibility for children inevitably involves a woman in a role which only she can fill. As a mother, a woman is both model and whipping boy (or girl). She must see that the children grow up to become free and responsible people, but she must also define limits and be there when she is needed—and all this whether the children are small or growing up. In purely practical respects, each stage in the children's lives is accompanied by its own worries and problems, but psychologically the responsibility is always equally heavy. Even if older children can manage the practical aspects of their lives extremely well on their own, they still need to feel sure of where they belong, and providing them with this sense of security requires both time and thought. Regardless of whether you are a single parent or living with a partner actively involved in the children's upbringing, the demands are inherent in the role of mother; they call for constant attention and a continual effort to adjust them in the best possible way to the other demands in a woman's life.

I have placed the mother role first simply because it still seems to be regarded as the most crucial one in a woman's life. The rest of the roles are not so easy to rank according to the importance ascribed to them, but there is no doubt that the career (or manager) role comes high on the list.

The manager role is always demanding, regardless of the sex of the manager. However, we have discussed in Chapter 4 the 'extra' demands that fall upon the woman manager. She becomes a model and spokesperson, and she has to be a mentor for her subordinates of both sexes. There are often no established models on which she can base her conduct in these roles; she has to develop her own style as she goes along, constantly improvising in new situations. This requires strength of character and, above all, the courage to develop a personal managerial role:

'When I first joined company X and was appointed marketing director it seemed as though everyone was pussy-footing round me, as though they were waiting for me to show them exactly who I was. The previous marketing director, a cheerful type in his forties, had been very popular. But when I really looked into how they'd been working I found there'd been an awful lot of carelessness and extravagance. I often had to be pretty tough at first, and I felt they regarded me as hard and pedantic. I often wanted to say to them all, "You don't know me as I really am. I've got to be like this, People are watching us, and I've got to show we can get results". But instead I gritted my teeth, and sometimes when I got home I wept. That's when they should have seen me, isn't it?'

MARGARETA, 38, Marketing Director

Even a boss has a boss (or bosses) and the relationship upwards also calls for much thought and hard work. Then there are colleagues with whom it is sometimes necessary to compete and/or collaborate. These relationships, too, require effort.

If we then add a whole range of 'private' roles (for instance, as partner, daughter, sister, and friend perhaps to both women and men) we soon realize just how many ties are calling for the time and attention of any one of us. Naturally, we sometimes have to accept the impossibility of meeting the demands of all these roles, even if we lower our sights, but however cleverly we choose between them, the feeling of inadequacy is difficult to overcome, and it gradually leads to frustration and stress.

All this may sound as though I accept the impossibility of combining a normal woman's life with a demanding and satisfying managerial role. Certainly, after talking to many women about this, I do have certain doubts, not least because the traditional managerial role does impose heavy restrictions on the 'where and when' of a person's life: managers must be available at work for so many hours, they have to meet certain people at agreed times even when they do not themselves consider the meetings to be particularly important. Thus various rituals and formal conventions traditionally involve a 10–12-hour working day, which inevitably leaves little time for the other roles or for the managers 'own' life:

'I don't think I'd feel so frustrated about having so little time for the children, if I didn't realise what an awful lot of time we waste at work. It feels so absurd to sit there marking time, when I think of all the things I could be doing instead. And then people are ridiculous about working late. We had a good example of this a few years ago. We'd just got a new managing director. He had just got divorced, and he often worked on until 8 or 9 in the evening. Of course he was new, and he wanted to learn the ropes I suppose, but I think he was also putting off the moment when he had to go home to his lonely flat. And believe it or not, everyone began to work late. It became the norm. People wanted to show how keen they were. Now the boss has married again and has a little boy; he goes home around 5 or 6, and so does everybody else. And our results are none the worse for it.'

KARIN, 45, *Accountant*

I have admitted to some doubt about the possibility of combining a normal female role with an exacting career, but I do not dismiss it altogether, for two reasons. One is that I badly want it to be possible, and I have met women who, despite all the difficulties, have proved that it is. The second reason stems from the results of recent research which has shown that women are at least as stress-resistant as men, if not more so, and that the different ways in which women and men react to the pressures of the 'achieving' world depend on learned behaviour patterns and social influences.

This seems to indicate that if the demands of the managerial world were intrinsically *human* rather than *male* then women and men would both find it easier to meet the demands and at the same time to live a fuller personal life. Instead of 'human' in the last sentence I could perhaps have said 'androgynous'.

Androgyny is a concept that has recently appeared in the debate on these topics, and it represents the wish to move away from the traditional male/female categorization and towards a new total picture of characteristics previously called 'manly' or 'womanly'. In the following section I shall be discussing the concept of the androgynous individual and considering how androgynous qualities can influence and be influenced by the demands of the more traditional managerial role and leadership style.

5.3 ANDROGYNOUS PEOPLE—WHO ARE THEY?

The word androgyny, from a combination of the Greek *andro* or man and *gyn* or woman, is as easy to explain as it is difficult to understand. That it is difficult to understand I have discovered whenever I have tried to introduce it into my lectures. Many people immediately associate it with bisexuality, transvestism and so on, but androgyny should not be regarded as the designation of a particular kind of person. It is a theoretical construction (or taxonomical class) based on the measurement of attributes *traditionally* classified as female or male. Androgyny is a type of psychological model, much like the traditional intelligence test which 'measures' certain qualities and then ranks people accordingly.

The underlying assumptions of the scientists who coined the concept of androgyny are (1) that every individual can possess both 'male' and 'female' attributes (in the *psychological* sense), (2) that traditional attitudes have previously determined what is designated as male or female in this respect, and (3) that these attitudes are moulded by our culture and our inherited sexual roles.

We can look at a simple illustration of this. Support that aggressiveness has always been regarded as a typically male characteristic. We construct a scale on which it can be measured and apply it to 100 boys and 100 girls. We get the unsurprising result that 80 of the boys and only 10 of the girls are very aggressive (according, that is, to our traditional scale). The question is, how should we classify the 20 boys and the 10 girls whose ratings diverge from the 'normal'? Are they simply at the tail end of the normal curve or would we get different results if we constructed a *new* measure of aggressiveness, based on the characteristics of these boys and girls?

With the help of this last method a scale has been designed for evaluating 'male' and 'female' behaviour and related attributes (Bem *et al.*, 1976). First, large groups of men and women were asked to indicate the characteristics that they considered desirable in a man or a woman. Naturally, too, they could also rate characteristics which they regarded as sex-neutral. In this way it was possible to identify attributes that were regarded as male or female according to traditional sex role thinking. Not very surprisingly, the following attributes attached to the male role: independence (standing alone), decisiveness (seeing fewer alternatives), willingness to take risks (not seeing the dangers), It was thought that the woman's role included being understanding (dependent), being helpful (indecisive), and affectionate (incapable ot breaking up). The characteristics in parentheses are what I regard as the mirror image of each attribute, i.e. the probable or possible description of the same characteristics as seen by the other sex. Once the scale based on traditional male and female characteristics had been obtained it was used to test another group of men and women. With the help of about 60 questions each person can obtain a new measure of the female and male elements in their own personalities. The Bem scale can provide a personal measure of both femininity and masculinity in both the traditional and the new sense. One person may have high ratings in one or the other or he or she may have high ratings in both, thus qualifying as *androgynous*. The traditional male role is associated with the desire to produce things, to get things done, while the traditional woman's role is geared largely towards personal relationships, caring, cherishing and so on. At least, this is how we usually put it, but I have often wondered why the creation of new members of the human race is not honoured with the classification 'production', while other activities which might well lead to the destruction of all mankind are always so termed. Bem's model, on the other hand, allows both women and men to acknowledge all their characteristics, and we then find that some people have always dared to ignore the limitations of traditional sex-stereotyping, seeking to develop a diversity of characteristics in contravention of current norms.

The newborn child, like a stretch of wild country whose potential is as yet all promise, provides an apt image here. Within the limits of the child's nature, he or she has every chance of becoming ... who knows? Later the restraints of upbringing and sexual typecasting begin to tame the original wild stretch of country, until finally only a little garden is left. Depending on whether the garden has been typecast as male or female, the child has been forced to grow inside a recognized fence within a specified enclosure. The androgynous individual is not so ready to accept the restrictions of this fence; rather, the androgynous among us allow all aspects of their potential to live on and develop to their fullest extent. Androgynous personalities may be both tough and sensitive, focusing on achievement as well as on human relationships, combining characteristics of the traditional male and female models as appropriate to their own natures.

It has long been considered unmanly to blush and unwomanly to fight. Yet it seems that the point is not whether some people can legitimately blush and some can legitimately fight; rather we should be asking ourselves exactly what restraints are preventing men as well as women from exploiting their original potential to the full. Nor from sheer laziness should we fall back uncritically on simplified models. It is here that the concept of androgyny has helped us to abandon our earlier rather blinkered view and to approach the whole question of manly or womanly behaviour with a fresh eye.

Androgynous individuals can orientate themselves towards achievement *and* human relationships. In other words, regardless of whether they are male or female (biologically speaking), they try to combine tradition and renewal, rationality and emotionality, conservation and growth, and in this they largely succeed. They are the new people and the new leaders.

Chapter 6

EXTERNAL CHANGES AND FUTURE ORGANIZATIONAL FORMS

As we have seen, there are many reasons why women do not become managers; so far we have looked at organizational conditions, what we could call the rules of the game, and have seen in them *one* important explanation. In this chapter I shall be considering several changes or trends in the world outside the organization, which in the not-too-distant future seem likely to generate new managerial roles and a new type of leadership. As an organizational form the traditional hierarchy has not favoured the presence of women as managers; in fact it would be nearer the truth to say that its rules have had a direct inhibiting effect on women's career chances. Could we then assume that other organizational forms would be more favourable to the recruitment of women managers and, if so, are there any signs of such forms becoming more common in the near future? It seems that there are.

6.1 CHANGES IN INFORMATION TECHNOLOGY

Many exciting developments are under way in the technological field and I shall be discussing only a small part of the overall picture, i.e. those trends which appear likely to have the greatest impact on organizational forms and the managerial roles of the future.

Much has been written about the appearance of the *information society*, but so far little appears to have been said about the organizational aspects of this revolution. It seems that the new information technology will be one of the crucial factors in the generation of different and more flexible organizational forms.

Information, communications and transactions have all recently adopted new forms and taken previously unknown paths with the exploitation of satellite communications, glass-fibre technology, computerized telephone systems, linked computer systems and cheap terminals. In offices, factories and homes, in cars and on boats, the new small computers are employed in all kinds of ways. In the office, every workplace can communicate with all the other workplaces not only by telephone but also via various types of terminals—word and text processors, copying machines, desk computers or television receivers. From a word processor a message is sent to a desk computer, or a text is sent to a copier in another part of the world. From his television set at home the financial director can check his company's bank accounts and give orders about disbursements or money transfers. In a hotel room on the other side of the world a salesman can use the telephone network and the hotel television to get news about orders, delivery capacity, and prices from his company's computer.

Telefax, Telex, Videotex, and Telepak are some of the mystifying names for communication between terminals, for the transfer of information from a computer to a terminal and vice versa, or for transactions such as money transfers from one computer to another. The various designations depend on the slightly different techniques used in the transfer of information, but the important point for any one computer, word processor or television receiver to communicate with all such machines. In the computer world they speak of systems and hardware being made 'compatible' with one another. It will be technically possible for every home and workplace to communicate with 'all' other homes and workplaces, in the same way that they do so with the major computer banks. Computer banks can provide more than mere figures and texts. Moving images, calculation programs and sounds are some related developments. It is we, and not the technology, that set the limits to communication in the new information society.

Another interesting product is the 'smart card', enabling a card reader in a computer anywhere in the world to take part in business transactions. The card is loaded with authorizations and rights, and can identify and legitimate the owner (for example, via a signature stored in electronic form).

Thus it is not only possible for us to communicate with one another via the electronic communication system; we can also design an organizational system with the authority and competence to make decisions about transfers. Authority and competence can also refer to the right of access to information systems and to order goods transport, the retrieval of goods from stock, or to simple matters such as booking a flight or a hotel room.

One of the main results of the new information technology is that it reduces distance in both time and space. This means that people can engage in global communication and the decision-makers do not necessarily have to gathered around the same table. It becomes easier to conduct business and transmit orders without the geographical restrictions that have always previously prevailed and which, to some extent, still do.

6.2 ROBOTIZATION

Microcomputers complete with software can be designed on a very small scale and included in machines based on systems of mechanical and hydraulic energy transfer, that is, in robots. These, which are appearing in increasing numbers in our factories and mines, at the bottom of the sea or in space, have very little in common with the huminoid beings of popular science fiction but they are capable of replacing a certain amount of human labour. A few man-like robots are certain to be made, if for no other reason than to amaze us all, but the decisive impact of the industrial robots will be felt mainly in working life. Attached to a production line or a wheeled truck, they can be programmed to carry out heavy or monotonous work such as assembling coachwork or tackling noxious tasks such as the lacquering of car bodies.

Hitherto industrial robots have been used mostly in industrial production of this kind, but even here they are still relatively few. However, towards the end of the 1980s they are expected to multiply and to appear in many other areas of industry and trade (for example, transport, energy extraction and mining). Their performance capacity will increase: they will be able to handle more—and more complex—phases in the various tasks, responding to external stimuli such as heat and making certain simple decisions such as introducing adjustments to maintain a constant temperature. It will also be possible to integrate them increasingly into the different components of the new information society, as they can be remote-controlled, reprogrammed or given new orders. They will also be capable of supplying reports from distant places.

Robots will be able to take over many of the tasks which at present are carried out by people, but the crucial point here is that the *control* of the robots will not be subject to any geographical limitation. Moreover, the traditional foreman function on the factory floor will become more or less superfluous: robots do not require the old type of supervision and their operations are subject to checking by self-surveillance. Leadership at the supervisor and foreman level has long been regarded as an important experience and a significant stage in a manager's career path. This is just one of the many things that robotization will change.

6.3 INTERNATIONALIZATION

Knowledge about the manufacture of iron took more than a thousand years to spread round the world. It took twenty years or so for television to establish itself in Europe, once it had become generally accepted in the United States. When Sony launched their 'freestyle' (Walkman) personal stereo in Japan, it took less

than a month to trigger a completely new type of listener behaviour throughout Western Europe and the United States. The
same kind of speeding-up has occurred in the communication of
news. During the Second World War radio was still providing the
quickest source of news; if we wanted to *read* what had happened
we had to wait for the newspapers perhaps a day or two later,
and to *see* the same events we had to rely on cinema newsreels,
which could take a few weeks longer. However, by the time of
the Vietnam war the whole world could watch in their armchairs
at home as events unfolded before their eyes.

International mass media systems have brought the continents
closer together. At the same time another system has been working in a similar direction, but not so visibly. If, say, I buy a pair
of shoes in a shop in Hong Kong and produce my credit card, the
assistant can immediately check whether I have enough money
in my account to be able to pay. Over the international computer
network the Hong Kong terminal can communicate with computers in Europe, where my credit limits and my latest balance are
registered.

In the same way the world of finance can record interest and
exchange rates, the prices of raw materials, and so on, which are
registered at once on terminals all over the world.

The shares of the large corporations are recorded worldwide on
all the major stock exchanges, in New York, London, Paris and
Tokyo. Ownership is also dispersed throughout the world. Finance
companies and banks combine in groups, which then acquire interests in a network of internationally operating companies. The
different countries are also interested parties, eager to attract employment and development projects to locations within their own
borders.

The world's major companies are globally owned, and they
have contacts and connections with governments, banks and finance companies. Governments, in turn, enter into trade agree-

ments with one another as part of a vast global network, and all this, together with information technology, tends to create a global society. The internationally composite nature of goods manufacture is just one example of this. A Swedish Volvo, for instance, may include Japanese computers, a French engine, Italian windscreen-wipers, Finnish tyres, an American gearbox, upholstery from Singapore, and coachwork made of Swedish steel. It may run on petrol from Kuwait and be fitted with a stereo from South Korea. Volvo is a product of the global production system, which in turn depends on the global finance system and information network.

It is obvious that a global society of this kind will make new demands on its business leaders and managers, if for no other reason because decision processes extend beyond national frontiers and are therefore subject to economic, political and social circumstances worldwide. This means that a future leader must be acutely aware of international conditions as well as being receptive to changes and cultural variations in the global setting.

6.4 THE EDUCATION EXPLOSION

Many writers and politicians have endeavoured to chart the future, and in particular to envisage 'future man'. Future studies have been required for social planning and for various other purposes, and instruments of varying accuracy have been developed for the projection of trends. At this point I must acknowledge the 'non-scientific' nature of my present approach: my argument is based mainly on impressions I have received from the many people with whom I have discussed these topics and from books I have read. I feel fairly certain that many of my 'guesses' would be supported by the findings of more scientifically organized studies. However, my intention here has been to provide examples of some of the most important and easily observable phenomena rather than to try to prove a particular hypothesis.

The generation born during the 1940s, the post-war young who will be taking over the leading posts in 10–20 years from now, seem to be revealing a rather special profile that distinguishes them from the established leaders of today. We are justified in claiming a new awareness for the members of this 'in-between' generation, those with one foot in the traditional world order and one firmly planted in the new. Among these people are the leaders of the near future. It is therefore of supreme importance to ask: What, essentially, have they learnt of leadership and development? What experiences have they had in the course of their maturing? In terms of socio-economic change, what influences have been at work upon them?

Probably the most invigorating social experience in most Western countries has been the education explosion. As living standards have risen, so has the level of education steadily increased. This applies to both sexes, even if the advances still take many men and women into different fields. However, in terms of level, there is little difference between sexes today, even in the fairly high age groups, in many countries.

Education greatly affects, and will continue to affect, the way in which we see ourselves and the world around us, including our fellow human beings. 'Vietnam', 'Watergate', 'Greenpeace"—these and similar movements or events have become familiar to so many people largely because a few individuals took upon themselves the intellectual responsibility of the opinion-leader or the informal leaders, spreading the message to those around them. The moral arguments of these enthusiasts of our own day are built on a more solid basis of fact than has ever been the case. Over the last 20 or 30 years we have seen the birth of diverse mass movements based almost entirely on voluntary involvement and private initiatives— something which would have seemed incredible before the Second

World War. The spread of ideas, and the mutual recognition of people who in the past would hardly have been aware of one another's existence or ambitions, is in one way a consequence of the new information technology we have been discussing. However, it has also acquired vital energy from a new focus, at least in the industrialized world, which has made people more observant, more willing to participate in social developments, and more aware of their own and other people's potential.

Various experiments in power-sharing and industrial democracy may or may not have 'succeeded', but the whole ideological debate on the co-determination issue has made a powerful impression. Few nowadays, regardless of political affiliation, would deny the importance of exploiting the individual's resources and inherent strengths in a world that must release all its creativity and positive motive forces if it is to survive.

Rising educational standards have also, we may hope, produced people more independent and better prepared to take a personal stand on what is right or wrong, good or bad. Blind obedience is gradually becoming a thing of the past, which means that leaders must be capable of putting forward their arguments and supporting their convictions more openly and effectively than ever before.

Whether it is the level of education itself or the greater awareness that it has generated, which makes the people of today (and tomorrow) demand the right to influence developments on both minor and major issues, is an open question. The fact remains that the individual is playing an increasingly important role even on questions of major import, and the interaction between women and men and their children has become a factor which must be understood and allowed for. Mature individuals will not accept standard solutions as to how they should live their lives; to them it is the search for a 'full' life which is meaningful, and this search includes a natural desire to be able to live a more rounded life, combining intellectual or practical skills with emotional needs, a life which has room for the balancing ingredients: career and private life, self-interest and caring. This is one reason why new qualities will certainly be needed in the leaders of the future; but it is equally certain that we shall be trying our new organizational forms. Those who have controlled our traditional hierarchies hitherto have done so with undeniable competence, but competence of another type will probably flourish when the hierarchy, as a structure, has outlived itself.

6.5 FUTURE ORGANIZATIONAL FORMS

Let us now recapitulate the most important of the trends discussed above, asking ourselves how they may favour—or even demand—the introduction of new organizational forms.

Promising conditions for the dispersal of operations traditionally bound to certain geographical locations are heralded by the *advances in information technology*. Working hours need no longer be as rigid as before; the necessary work can be done at different times and in different places. Those who are accountable for results can therefore remain more flexible, organizing their work along individual lines. Rapid and effective communications render unnecessary much of the travelling that has to be undertaken today. It is becoming possible to present collections or conduct negotiations without bringing all those involved together in one place. These are a few examples of the direction in which things are moving.

Control can be simplified in various ways with the help of the new techniques. Many routine administrative functions will disappear. All this is likely to affect the traditional hierarchy on two counts. First, operations can be split more easily among separate units, which can then organize their work to suit themselves, provided they maintain a satisfactory level of performance. Second, centralized staffs of specialists will be able to play an even more important role than they do today, serving a multitude of scattered units, perhaps even entering the market outside their own organization.

A company's training or computer department, for example, might be detached to become an independent company selling its services not only to its former colleagues but also in competition on the open market. This should bring fresh vigour and efficiency into many staffs and specialist groups which today lead sheltered lives inside large protective corporations. Thus while hierarchy splits up into an array of independent units (decentralization) the new information and communication systems provide better opportunities for effective control and, consequently, for combining and mobilizing more units than ever before (concentration).

Robotization cannot fail to affect future production arrangements and, in particular, workplaces. Previously, people and machines were brought together at a particular place, in specific workshops, where the manufacture of goods was then possible. Future production will consist increasingly of assembly processes, with parts gathered from many different locations. Locality will no longer be a given factor; various stages in the assembly process may even be transferred from one place or one country to another, as seems most effective in economic or political terms at any particular moment. Profitability, combined with social and political opportunities, will be more important than it is today in determining whether various parts of the production process should be located. A robot is international in the sense that it is steered by the same language wherever it may be. No foremen or supervisors of the traditional kind are needed. Specialists and service personnel are necessary, but not actual surveillance. Rather, staff specialists can work in 'shifts' in various parts of the world. Specialist teams will probably evolve, prepared to sell emergency services and other types of expertise to different companies on the market.

The envisaged factory of the future, geographically flexible and requiring no human supervision on the shopfloor, provides further opportunities for decentralization and the launching of project units. Perhaps future companies will be able to adjust size or production arrangements more quickly and effectively to market demands, just because they have no need to own and invest in production machinery that is inevitably bound to a particular location or to assume responsibility for a workforce tied to a particular place.

Developments on the financial markets and in the banking system are pointing in the same direction. Once, some sort of *material asset* was required for starting up a new operation. Today, ideas and knowledge are probably enough, and in future will almost certainly be so; the rest will be rented, leased or borrowed, given the necessary administrative capacity to make the whole thing work and the business flair for selling the product at a profit. This brings us back to *internationalization* and *training*.

Great competence is required of anyone operating successfully not only outside their own country but also outside their own area of expertise. The industrial leaders of today often started their careers in some particular branch of specialized knowledge, perhaps within technology and/or economics. As their responsibilities increased they gradually grew into their roles as international businessmen and statesmen. The authorities on the domestic front have remained firmly entrenched in a norm system determined by the current educational set-up and by the practical experience acquired on the rungs of the career ladder. The businessman and industrial leader of the future will face many demands of quite another kind.

Working in a global perspective, while also seeing that many small scattered parts continue to pull together, calls for talents of a special kind. Since formal education and research often lag behind reality, we shall have to look to the practitioners all over the world to show us the new styles of leadership and managerial roles that we shall have to cultivate.

Chapter 7

TOWARDS A NEW LEADERSHIP STYLE

Only those who have fully found themselves in this world can realize their natures. Only those who realize their natures can lead other natures to self-realization. Only those who lead other natures to self-realization can realize the nature of things.

This quotation from Tzu-Ssu, a grandson of Confucius, contains the essence of what the word 'leadership' suggests to me. Over the last ten years or so, many writers, educators and consultants have turned their attention to the question of leadership, not least perhaps because they have recognized the money to be earned from a countless variety of leadership courses.

The unkind view could be that these organizers intentionally exploit the mystique and glamour of the leader role in order to attract people to their own particular courses, people cherishing a secret dream of success, of one day becoming a charismatic leader. Many courses are nominally addressed to existing leaders, but in my experience it is rarely the real leaders who attend them; it is much more likely to be the young high-fliers or middle-level managers who are most eager to take part. What are they hoping to learn? What is it that attracts them about 'leadership'? It is not only training courses which have flourished in the wake of the leadership cult; innumerable books, both scientific and popular, have been written about leadership and leaders. In recent years best-sellers introducing some new leadership philosophy have appeared in the United States every six months. It is simply a matter of choosing whether you want to adopt 'walk-around management', 'sit-down-and-talk management', 'only-go-by-crisis management', 'one-minute management', or 'never-say-goodbye management'. The list could be continued *ad infinitum*. One minute we are told not to let people into our offices, but to walk around all day patting people on the back, talking to them and discussing their problems according to a special schedule.

The next we are told to stay in our offices and to let people come to see us and to tell us (preferably without sitting down) what they have on their minds; if they are allowed to sit, they will take too long and may wander from the point.

A few pearls of wisdom may lie concealed in these books, but most of their messages can probably be dismissed as fashionable gimmicks, quickly losing any power to inspire new approaches to leadership. Many writers have tried to establish typologies of the personalities of 'the leaders'; these attempts are certainly not without interest, but unfortunately they often focus on one particular person and consequently tend to create heroic stereotypes whose leadership styles cannot simply be copied, however successful they may be.

Although it is thus difficult to chart leader personalities and leadership styles in a way that is both intelligent and meaningful we have to acknowledge the necessity of trying. We may, after all, learn something about getting people to collaborate with one another in the achievement of common goals, or about the qualities which up to now have characterized those who become leaders. This last point has an immediate bearing on one of the main questions I have been asking in this book: why are there so few women leaders?

7.1 'ONLY THOSE WHO HAVE FULLY FOUND THEMSELVES IN THIS WORLD CAN REALIZE THEIR NATURES'

Ancient philosophers taught that only by knowing ourselves can we know others, and no-one is likely to deny that adequate self-knowledge and good self-insight are necessary to the achievement of personal maturity. However, does the established leader role in the traditional hierarchy allow people to realize their natures?

Are not certain parts of the individual's 'nature' allowed to flourish, while others are supposed to be suppressed or at least firmly kept in check? In Chapters 4 and 5 we saw how strong male-dominated norms interact with the structure of the hierarchy, and how in almost all organizations the stated norms are one thing while those that actually steer behaviour are quite another.

Today's leaders have learnt to live in two worlds. They communicate with their subordinates on two levels: the words are democratic but the feelings are authoritarian. The leaders of our time must learn to know themselves. How can we achieve self-insight, how dare we realize our natures, if, according to tacit agreement, no emotions should appear or even exist, and if the ideal is to clench our teeth, but up a bold front, and reject any sign of weakness?

During the 1970s 'unfreeze' or consciousness-raising courses for managers became extremely popular, particularly in the United States. The idea was that people should be given an opportunity to learn to know themselves by allowing their hidden emotions to come to the surface. Everything, from rather frivolous 'cuddle' courses to more sophisticated exercises in group-dynamics, was fashionable. Sensitivity became a familiar concept. I was and still am sceptical of methods like these. Intelligent adults cannot be changed by a few days' attendance on a residential course. The whole thing begins to seem like a game, but a game that can have unpleasant consequences for people unable to cope with such self-confrontation.

So is it impossible to alter the organizational setting in such a way as to allow leaders, or indeed all participants, to become whole and mature? In our earlier discussion of androgyny I suggested that certain 'androgynous' leaders would be capable of allowing a greater number of qualities to mature and flourish and of accepting a wider range of 'normal' behaviour. Unfortunately, the androgynous managers seem to be very rare today, just as the number of women managers brave enough to break with established conformist leadership styles is sadly small.

7.2 'ONLY THOSE WHO REALIZE THEIR NATURES CAN LEAD OTHER NATURES TO SELF-REALIZATION'

'To lead other natures to self-realization' seems to me to be the very essence of good leadership, but how often is leadership based on principle? Today, perhaps not very often; but given the new requirements that the organizational forms of tomorrow will bring, leadership must surely find its strength in the personal freedom to grow, and in voluntary participation rather than in control. The leader's main task will be to help other people to assume responsibility for their own development and growth and for the efficiency of the operations in which they are engaged. But how can people be encouraged to realize their own potential?

First and foremost, a culture has to be created that allows for individual learning and experimentation. As we have already noted, almost all companies declare themselves willing to encourage creativity and commitment in their employees, but very few of them manage to live up to their words. Why? Argyris (1976) discusses in some detail the difference between the explicit and implicit norms of an organization, and coins the expressions 'espoused theories' and 'theories in use'. He finds that people are often unaware of the gap between these, and suggests that the first step towards changing the prevailing norms must be to make people conscious of the discrepancy. By first identifying the norms or values which people claim to support and then watching their behaviour as it reveals the norms and values that in fact determine what they do we can find a basis for developing new norms and changing established behaviours.

Argyris has revealed a number of general norms that often appear to govern behaviour in hierarchies, regardless of what the espoused norms may say. Some of these are as follows:

(1) People want to define for themselves the nature of their situation and the goals that are to apply, even if they claim to be doing so as part of a 'democratic' process.
(2) Neither they themselves nor other people should show emotion.
(3) The intellectual aspects of a problem are to be emphasized and the emotional ingredients played down. In support of these basic ambitions, people employ unilateral behaviour strategies, such as fighting for their own ideas and trying to stop other people from doing the same.

Constructive alternatives to these norms could be:

(1) Help people to generate useful and true information.
(2) Make well-founded decisions on the basis of this information.

The source of these norms is a conviction that effective behaviour and learning is only possible if people possess reliable (true) information, if they are competent in their field and are prepared to accept responsibility, and if they are willing to reassess continually the effectiveness of their own and other people's decisions.

If such norms and values are allowed to govern behaviour it should become possible to release two constructive capacities, neither of which are unusual but which in combination are rare: one is the ability to inspire support for one's own ideas, and the other the ability to encourage questioning and criticism of all ideas, including one's own.

In Argyris's (1982) view, a manager who has the courage to reveal all aspects of his nature, and who lets his subordinates reveal theirs, should also be capable of solving the seven dilemmas of power:

(1) How to be strong while also acknowledging the dilemmas that surround us.
(2) How to assert our opinions without becoming dominant.
(3) How to fight for our ideas while encouraging others to question them.
(4) How to deal constructively with our subordinates' fears when we are also afraid.
(5) How to live with our own fears while asking other people to overcome theirs and to act more openly.
(6) How to exploit fear as a way of achieving greater understanding.
(7) How to get people to believe that we genuinely want to change our leadership style when we ourselves are still uncomfortable with the 'new' one.

Any resolution of the dilemmas of power seems to call for a truly competent and well-integrated personality; respect for other people has to be based on self-respect and a clearsighted sense of one's own integrity. In my experience, people who doubt their own competence are generally those who cling to a formal position and the superficial symbols of power as a basis for authority and prestige, while those whose authority springs from genuine competence have no need to leap to the defence of position and prestige, but instead can allow and even encourage other people to realize themselves. I suggested above that the norm prescribing the suppression of emotion can have a deeply inhibiting effect on learning. Some readers may feel that, on the contrary, emotions should be kept under control, and that emotionality may even inhibit a rational approach. Without embarking on too philosophical a discussion, I should perhaps reply to this putative argument.

There is, of course, an emotional aspect in any behaviour between people, but it is not this general type of 'personal chemistry' that is interesting in our present context so much as the defence mechanisms and negative reactions that jeopardize effective cooperation. People who have to work every day in an atmosphere of contradictory messages will react with suspicion and feelings of impotence, which they will then try to conceal in various ways. This will generate even more mental tension and a distancing of the self from the job, from colleagues, and from the organization. Alienation is perhaps too strong a word here, but we can all recall examples of how suspicion and fear ultimately led to pretence and self-deception, both of which are effective barriers to learning and creativity. What is more, if a further norm gradually becomes accepted, namely that such negative tensions should also be concealed, then we end up in a world 'where everyone knows that everyone knows', but nobody is brave enough to reduce the negative process. Argyris describes an example of this mechanism:

> Mistakes and deviations from plans are camouflaged by employees who firmly follow the 'accepted' organizational rules and play along in all the defensive games. The cover-up depends on games geared to the idea that mistakes must never come out, and the existence of such games depends on the existence of other games that pretend there *are* no games ... The following is an example of the sort of reasoning that occurs. In our company we have a product X that is the apple of management's eye and which represents the great hope for the future. In fact it is full of faults and is difficult to sell— we should never have invested in it. But as we never admit to making mistakes, we have to do everything we can to hide

98

the fact that the product X is no good. But of course no-one
must *see* that we are pretending. We have to pretend that we
are not pretending ...

A good organizational culture embracing a healthy team spirit
combined with respect for the competence and needs of every
member will favour individual growth and development as well
as effectiveness and the achievement of organizational goals. To
generate a good organizational culture is the foremost responsibility of the leader.

As a consultant I have often encountered an exaggerated conviction that the only really effective way of creating a good organization is to choose the right team. If we can only find the
right man for the right post, then everything else will follow.
This seems to be a potentially dangerous argument. First, few
managers are ever in a position to choose *all* their staff but
have to make do with whomever is there; second, people all
possess a variety of competences, including many strengths and
weaknesses, and 'new' competences can emerge from interactions
or combinations between different members of the team. It is
for just this reason that every member should be seen as a resource, and an environment should be created in which they can
grow.

Finally, a consultancy case of my own provides an apt illustration. Company X, a high-technology export firm, decided to
invest some of their money in women and to recruit a few more
female technicians. Of course, they had to be clever girls. A lively
recruiting campaign was launched at several universities in order
to find fresh graduates in certain relevant fields.

Two candidates fulfilled the requirements: two young women
around 25 years old. The company was particularly pleased to
have found two of them: they would be able to support each
other, which would perhaps prevent adjustment problems in the

R & D department where they were to work. They could form a little group of their own and show what they could do.

When the women had been working there for two years I was called in: there were difficulties in the R & D department. Dissatisfaction was rife; the manager had suffered a heart attack and, worst of all, the women were not nearly as efficient as people had hoped. One of them was frequently off sick and the other rarely produced anything worthwhile. What had happened?

My analysis of the problems revealed the following. The manager of R & D had worked his way up through the company. He was 55 years old, an engineer trained at technical college, and possessing a talent for administration which had hitherto helped him to keep within his R & D budget. However, he had never taken any active part in the relatively independent work of the project groups.

When the women joined the department he had been pretty worried. Not that he had anything against women, but how was he supposed to act towards these well-educated girls, young enough to be his daughters? Nor was he sure what they were meant to be good at. How would the others (all men between 25 and 35) react? He decided that he must not be too soft, he must be careful not to show the women any favouritism. Yet if he did what management wanted, immediately assigning them to a project, the others who had had to start from the bottom in an established team would be furious. He could just imagine them asking, 'Why haven't they had to struggle like we did, why should they get a project straight away? They're only just out of school.' No, perhaps he ought to start them off on something fairly simple, jobs that had to be done that were not all that important, then he could see what they were worth. Naturally, he would not have dared to talk about this to anyone else in the department, least of all to the girls themselves. To them he simply said: 'We'll have to see; something is sure to turn up soon, but for the moment ...'

Two years later the women had given up. Management was disappointed: the women did not seem to have started any exciting projects; had it been a mistake to recruit them after all? The atmosphere in the department deteriorated. The manager felt the strain, the womens' disenchantment was beginning to spread.

It was in fact a typical story: a change had been launched without any real preparation and with negative consequences, all because no-one had considered the prevailing culture or the manager's norms, which were challenged by this change so lightly undertaken. The sudden appearance of a new kind of member in his team left the manager feeling unsure and confused, but because the prevailing norms told him to look strong and invulnerable he was prevented from acknowledging and tackling the problems immediately. Thus the difficulties simply went on growing until neither he nor anyone else in the department could handle them.

We could, of course, have been brutal, and said 'He's just a bad manager', but it was not so simple. He was in fact a good one, so long as his world was secure and his accustomed behaviour worked. When the change occurred he became a bad manager, but it was the responsibility of his superior to see that the prevailing norms and culture were of such a kind that the R & D manager would be able to tackle the problems openly and without fear, rather than concealing them as long as he possibly could. In an open creative culture this case would never have arisen.

7.3 'ONLY THOSE WHO LEAD OTHER NATURES TO SELF-REALIZATION CAN REALIZE THE NATURE OF THINGS'

So far we have been discussing leadership in relation to individuals and to the norms governing the individual's opportunities for development, although I have perhaps also implied some connection between personal creativity and the innovativeness of the organizations in which people work. However, when we turn to 'realizing the nature of things' we shall have to shift our perspective and consider leadership on a meta-level.

An organization always exists in a particular environment and operates on a particular market. The norms steering the actions of the organizational totality *vis-à-vis* its environment and its operations on the market can be described as its *strategy*. Is there any connection between internal leadership (the organizational culture) and strategy in relation to the surrounding world (i.e. the environment and the market)? Can a company ultimately survive with a divided stance towards its surrounding or does economic survival and expansion depend on a state of harmony between 'internal' and 'external' norms, i.e. the norms that govern behaviour towards the world outside? I am convinced that such harmony is vitally important, and it seems that, in the real world, companies which succeed in acting progressively and which are genuinely capable of realizing 'the nature of things' are those that have understood this necessity.

Let us examine a few examples. IKEA is widely recognized as a successful Swedish and multinational company. I have no inside knowledge of what their strategy has been, but the story of their success runs as follows. In part of the Swedish province of Smaland some people were skilled at making cane chairs; they made them better and more cheaply than anyone else. Their operations expanded and they began to make sofas, tables and beds. Other competence was called in, in the shape of designers, publicity experts, and so on. At the same time the company continued to send out the original message: 'We are the best because we come from Smaland where people are thrifty, pertinacious and industrious, and we believe in our employees. At the same time we recognize that the new competence and the new ideas that have been introduced must be allowed to develop and measure themselves against fresh challenges.' Experts in textiles were recruited, and suddenly it was possible for the company to produce its own materials, so why not include these in the product range? The underlying philosophy also focuses genuinely on the customer: the customer is clever enough to assemble his own furniture, at any rate with the right kind of support from IKEA. Therefore someone who could not otherwise have afforded a new bookshelf can become an IKEA customer by contributing much of the necessary labour himself. The whole process has developed into a philosophy *vis-à-vis* market and customers, still building essentially on the original straightforward internal norm. Roughly speaking, IKEA is saying: 'You build your own setting; we supply the building blocks!' Thus the company has succeeded in developing a market philosophy from an internal one: not only are they selling bookshelves to assemble at home, they are also selling a life-style. Their strategy, however it may have been worded, has certainly been effective, and there must have been many positive learning experiences in the kind of leadership that led to the goal.

From my own experience I can quote an example, which must remain anonymous, in which the internal and external leadership and strategic thinking were *not* in accord. An established and prestigious high-tech company, based originally on a stroke of inventive genius, found itself struggling in an increasingly difficult market. They decided to look for some new product ideas by organizing a new department to be known as the 'experiment factory'. This was to be no ordinary research and development department; instead its manager was given wide powers to organize the work of the department as an independent unit within certain broad budgetary limits. However, nobody allowed for the fact that the people who were to work there would be coming from different parts of the organization with different subcultures, and that they would therefore find it difficult to start collaborating with one another in completely new conditions. Nor would they be able to abandon the established game rules and suddenly start acting independently, as though they were running a business of their own. Old loyalties have deep roots, and without any real profit responsibility it was, anyway, difficult to agree on effective ways of working. Management soon discovered that although the experiment factory had delivered a hundred or so 'new' ideas, none of these were deemed likely to survive as viable products on the market by decision-makers in the traditional hierarchy. What was wrong? Were the ideas as bad as they seemed, or was the parent hierarchy suspicious of the new fangled factory and eager to prove that its ideas were impossible? Would the product ideas survive in a different organizational setting, or were the people in the experiment factory so anxious to create an individual norm system, despite the difficulties, that they became unrealistic and lost their commercial sense?

My analysis suggested several explanations for the relative failure of the experiment factory, of which the most important was that it was expected to function as an autonomous unit, as indeed it did. However, because it lacked contact with both the market and customers its ideas were often unrealistic. As management became aware of this they eventually agreed to grant the experiment factory greater independence. It became an autonomous company, testing its own product, assessing the markets, and so on.

This case shows how difficult it is to introduce new norms. Here, people accustomed to a hierarchy were suddenly asked to function as entrepreneurs and inventors. The company's external image was also such as to make it appear bureaucratic and authoritarian in the eyes of its employers.

It will rarely be possible to introduce any radical change in a company's internal culture without at the same time adjusting external strategy—a fact that has been recognized by many companies which have successfully altered their corporate profile.

7.4 THE ORGANIZATIONAL FORMS AND LEADERSHIP STYLES OF TOMORROW

In Chapter 6 we looked at some changes in the environment which are likely to affect future organizational forms. Because of technological innovation, internationalization, and various social changes in education and other fields, traditional hierarchies may not continue to provide the most efficient structure. Instead there will probably be a number of fluctuating network organizations, composed and recomposed to answer specific needs. Such networks will require a more democratic type of control, and management's main role will be to ensure the necessary ' collaboration based on competence and skill.

Because of the tendency towards concentration which we noted above, management will have to be capable of creating an internal and external philosophy allowing for contributions from different cultures. Large multinational corporations such as IBM, VISA, General Motors and so on have shown us that corporate strategies must be capable of extending beyond national cultures while also allowing for local or national norms and values. The pressures on tomorrow's leaders will thus be considerable. They will have to be able to identify and interpret different personal needs among staff and customers. In other words, they will have to be receptive, in both social and human terms. They will have to be 'statesmen' as well as experts in more than one field, since they may well have to combine technological development and creativity with an ability to provide a 'learning environment' for their subordinates and colleagues. I have already suggested rather boldly that blind obedience may soon be a thing of the past, which means that people will have to be motivated and inspired to work together of their own free will towards a common goal.

How will this affect women? Will there be more leaders and managers than there are at present? Many male business leaders today ask why they 'must' invest in women. 'Give me one reason,' they say, 'why more women managers would make any real or interesting difference.' Best of all, they would like a calculus demonstrating the commercial benefit of such a move. I generally keep quiet in situations like this, partly because it cannot at present be demonstrated that women managers would behave very differently from men, and partly because the question has been wrongly put. If we assume that the intelligence of a population follows a normal curve and is independent of sex, and if we also assume that men and women reach the same educational standard in most Western countries, how can we afford to deny ourselves the gifts and creativity lodged in half the population? How can we afford *not* to exploit this competence in a meaningful way? This is where I feel that the still-unrevealed demands that will be made on the leaders of the future may well serve the women's cause.

Because the new information technology and other advances will allow for more flexible managerial roles, and because various other changes including the internationalization of business, will call for human qualities such as social and verbal ability and the capacity to develop others in a diversified corporate culture, it seems likely that more managers will be women in future. Not because women are better at listening or at learning languages, for example, but simply because with the growing demands on competence and creativity we will no longer be able to afford not to recruit among the whole population.

Chapter 8

DEVELOPING YOUR COMPANY AND YOUR WORKFORCE

In Chapter 7 I suggested that the most important element in the new leadership involves the creation of a setting in which people can learn and grow. The title of this chapter—'Developing your company and your workforce' instead of 'Developing your workforce and your company'—has thus not been chosen at random. Rather, it is an expression of my conviction that you cannot develop an organization except by developing its personnel. The workforce is often a company's most expensive resource, as well as generally its most irreplaceable. However, by personnel development I mean much more than merely training and career-planning in the traditional sense. I am saying that we should also consider the position of the leadership at all levels, and the culture which that leadership generates throughout the organization. I am also suggesting that the internal culture must be in harmony with the strategy and goals employed by the company in dealing with its markets and the world in which it operates.

8.1 HOW CAN NEW NORMS BE CREATED?

Without a coherent strategy which employees can understand and with which they can identify it will be difficult to develop a cohesive and viable internal culture. The corporate strategy must be comprehensible, and it must be seen as a natural part of the internal culture. If it is to be so regarded, then employees at all levels must be involved in its creation and operation.

Yet, how often do we find that strategic thinking is the preserve of the top brass! Conferences and meetings with titles such as 'Policies for the future' or 'Strategic planning' are not usually attended by anyone below the highest rungs on the ladder, while people at lower levels are expected to work to more concrete short-term goals. These last are certainly every bit as important, but ideally both perspectives are needed at every level.

If all its members are to take an active part in strategic thinking a company must have an effective management capable of creating an environment in which creativity and learning are not only allowed but are even encouraged. Such an environment is likely to be characterized by openness, honesty, and efficient communications. How can such an atmosphere be made to penetrate every corner of the organization? One thing at least is certain: there will be no genuine openness or honesty unless the espoused norms agree with the norms in use. If the discrepancy between what is said and what is actually done is too great, learning will not thrive (cf. Chapter 7). Further, if people perceive messages as false or dishonest they will react with fear and suspicion and other defensive behaviour. In such an atmosphere effective communication becomes impossible.

Thus it is vital that the norms prevailing at the top are also applied consistently at all other levels in the organization; and it is in this context that the leaders (or managers) can play a vital role. Feedback is an overworked term for a necessary ingredient in the communication process. Without feedback there is no learning. Also, feedback must operate in both directions, upwards and downwards in the organization. In other words, direct and effective communications depend on a continual dialogue between managers and other employees. For purely routine decisions and tasks, simple accepted rules of thumb may be adequate. With important decisions related to motivation and the release creativity we should think in terms of a *process* in which everyone is involved—granted that roles will differ somewhat, depending on competence, experience and power. Leaders possess power and must, of course, use it; but if the use of power precludes any possibility of questioning the decisions taken, its effect will be suffocating. Leaders must be able to use power in the right way: they must have the courage to let people (including themselves) question their decisions and the way in which they are using their power.

Feedback includes positive responses such as praise, appreciation and rewards, and negative responses such as criticism and punishment. It is very important to be able to explain one's reactions to a particular performance, for only in this way can people learn successively from their successes and failures. In the studies described in Chapter 1 one complaint emerged on which almost all the women agreed, namely that they never received enough feedback from their bosses—something which in the long run must damage relations between the two parties.

Working on management training programmes (for male managers) I have often found people admitting to a great element of fear and uncertainty on this point.

'You may think this is ridiculous, but once I was so angry with Birgit for losing an important customer that I really bawled her out. And then something happened which always makes me nervous—she burst into tears and rushed out of the room. She was off sick for a couple of days. When she came back, everything seemed normal, but I felt embarrassed. I must never let my feelings run away with me again, I thought. But at the same time I'd lost some of my old confidence in her. Damn it all, it's not professional to cry and carry on like that.'

SVEN, 48, *Sales Manager*

My question to Sven was: 'Is it professional, not daring to say to Birgit when she came back: "Birgit, you know I can't cope when people cry, it makes me nervous. But now it's happened, let's talk about it, shall we?"'

However, if male managers often lack the courage to provide direct open criticism they seem to find it even more difficult to give praise or show appreciation in a way that women can understand.

I should perhaps add that they are not always successful with their male subordinates either (cf. Chapters 2 and 3); but with women they are particularly inadequate:

> 'I wondered for ages how I could possibly ask Richard [her boss] what he really thought about me launching the equal opportunities project on my own, with the support of the personnel department and the union. Did he really think it was irrelevant to us in the design department? There aren't so many of us [women who had been promoted] here, so it might have been more natural for some other department to take it up. In the end, when I finally asked him, all he said was "Oh, it's all right." What did he mean? Was it a good thing or not?'
>
> ANNE, 42, *Design Engineer*

It is astonishing how much energy people spend, guessing and interpreting and trying to understand one another in situations like this. The whole problem could probably be solved fairly easily if people would only sit down together and discuss what has happened, giving one another their own pictures of events and then trying to agree on a workable *modus vivendi*.

Obviously you do not try to telephone someone if the wires have been cut; it should be equally obvious that you cannot send a message by a faulty communications system, particularly if it concerns something as important and sensitive as the creation of new norms. You must be patient and allow all the time that is needed; and you must check the means of transmission before you start. In the present context this means ensuring a common language and mutual trust.

Thus the first and most important step in any attempt to develop new norms for the promotion of an open and creative organizational culture is to consider carefully the present state of affairs. In the language of consultancy we can call this making the diagnosis. How do people in the company communicate with one another? What methods do they use, how often do they communicate, and how well to they understand? Only when we have answers to these questions should we proceed to the next step, namely setting up a dialogue which can lead to the generation of new norms.

My experience as a consultant unfortunately suggests that although business leaders are interested in change and eager to introduce what is 'new' as quickly as possible, they are not so willing to look at the way things are now. 'After all,' they seem to be saying, 'we know things aren't so good at present.' However, we must begin by looking at the present state of affairs, at where we stand *now*, before taking the plunge into something new.

8.2 INTEGRATED PERSONNEL DEVELOPMENT

It may not be so difficult to create little 'Volvo-ites' at Volvo or 'MacDonalds folk' at MacDonalds, but how long can we expect the creation to last? If we choose to send messages along a faulty line we may succeed for a while, but the success will be fragile and the 'message' unlikely to survive for long.

Many companies have been inspired by the service concept, for instance: if SAS has done so well from its service courses, perhaps there would be something in it for us? Certainly there may be, but *not* if we rush eagerly into launching a new idea quickly and without due preparation. Rather, we should have the self-discipline to make haste slowly, giving ourselves time to work on the idea and to harmonize it with our corporate culture and the habits of mind of our people. This, unfortunately, is often much more difficult.

We only have to look at the many equal opportunities projects that have been launched. These often include well-designed programmes and clear goals (on paper) and a reasonable (i.e. tight) budget. Why do they so rarely lead to any *concrete* changes?

The will is there, and models for how we should proceed. All the necessary conditions may be fulfilled, and yet nothing happens. Why not? Simply because we have isolated and encapsulated this one activity; we expect to solve everything neatly but without setting the problem in its true context as part of the meaningful continuation and survival of the operation as a whole. In a shipwreck at sea a gentlemanly norm applies—'women and children first' (perhaps to ensure reproduction?)—but when a company is heading for the rocks then 'women and children' get the last places in the lifeboats. Why?

The very expression 'integrated personnel development' implies the indivisibility of this process: different policy issues must be tackled simultaneously and in parallel. Above all, there must be a coherent underlying philosophy, and one which is so firmly entrenched that the appearance of new and possibly important goals or values need not be regarded as a threat. There is sufficient scope for them to compete with existing ideas; or at least there are opportunities for an open discussion of their possible position in the established culture. A system of integrated personnel development would make it impossible to run an equal opportunities project while also conducting management training courses designed and steered by other norms and other people. Integrated staff development means taking each individual person seriously and sending the same message to everyone, though possibly not always expressed in exactly the same way. Above all, there must be a clear link between what is done about one strand in corporate policy and what is done about another.

In many companies equality issues have become a trial of strength between management and unions, a development which has definitely not benefited women. Because of the design of the sex-discrimination law on the Swedish labour market (cf. Chapter 1) people are too inclined to make a bargaining issue of the problem. However, I feel intuitively that this is the wrong approach. To begin with, unions and shop stewards are not better representatives of the women at a workplace than the women themselves could be and, second, the question of sex equality tends to become a controversial union issue which has to compete with other 'causes' for the attention and sympathy of the union members. I have taken part in equal opportunities studies among workers in the food industry, and it seems that the women's problems are much the same on the shopfloor, in the service departments, or in management. It is always assumed that men can speak for women—and men do. However, great integrity and courage are called for if people are to represent a group of which they are not members, and it is not all shop stewards who are blessed with these qualities—on the contrary. Then there is the risk of 'trading', of playing off one group against the other, and history unfortunately shows that even when women are in the majority on the shopfloor they still fail to assert their rights and opinions through the medium of the shop stewards.

In a genuinely integrated system of personnel development the old established games between different seats of influence must be abandoned; in fact we should even go so far as to *expose the conflicts* and analyse them seriously before proceeding to formulate new game rules for developing the necessary dialogue. Naturally, the company's strategy *vis-à-vis* its environment and its potential for survival also represent a vital element in this analysis, which is exactly why it is so important not to assign 'strategic' problems exclusively to certain levels in the company.

Instead, in some way or another people at all levels should be involved in strategy formulation. Integrated personnel development means that all the members of a company are regarded as equally valuable partners in the dialogue. If this goal is realized, the organization will also acquire a team of loyal and unselfish members.

8.3 COMPANY GEISHAS OR PARTNERS ON EQUAL TERMS?

Many workplaces today have equal numbers of men and women. However, segregation ensures that the female half of the work-force is not being exploited as best it could. Nor is it only the women who are dissatisfied with this arrangement; the male managers, too, are aware of pressure from their female staff and from women's groups. It seems that many men, today's managers, are seriously concerned to find new models for a better environment for the female members of their workforce, recognizing at the same time that this will generate a more efficient and creative organization. Here, too, there is a danger in proceeding too quickly. If these managers decide to promote a few women but do not also carefully prepare the way, the result may be a serious setback to the women concerned and even to the idea as a whole.

If as a result of external and internal pressure business leaders decided to impose a kind of quota system, I am not at all sure that women would ultimately benefit. They are only too likely to find themselves in roles where their traditional female qualities constitute the reason for their appointment; they become the company's geishas. The step from this to a system in which the individual's competence is the major deciding factor is indeed a long one.

Countless business leaders have expressed the hope that women would bring new life and fresh ideas into their companies. Of course, they are right: women could do this. If, however, women feel they have been chosen because of certain 'womenly' qualities which they may possess, rather than for the competence which they *know* they possess, then their reaction will be sharply negative. They will see themselves as a kind of hostage, as captives of the very stereotype from which they have sought to escape by acquiring the training and qualifications which they thought would guarantee assessment and selection 'on equal terms'.

Even the most sympathetic business leader can make comments like the following:

'I really want more women in top management. But up to now I've been disappointed in their contribution—those who've had a chance to show what they can do. There's been nothing very remarkable, at least nothing different from what the boys could do. If only they would exploit their personalities more, I think they could do quite a lot on the selling side, for example.'

PAUL, 53, *Managing Director*

I suggest that if women are subjected to such expectations then women managers will fall into the kind of trap described in Chapter 5, which will benefit neither them nor their companies. If, however, a company seriously wants to promote equal opportunities, if it wants to abolish the differences between women and men at all levels, what should it do?

For many years I have been helping various companies and other organizations to design and implement equal opportunities projects. Some of these have actually led to change; others, launched mainly as a sop to public opinion and lacking any wholehearted support, have not. In the following section I shall describe the course of one of the more successful projects.

8.4 AN INTEGRATED EQUALITY PROJECT AT COMPANY X

Interviews with women on the factory floor, as part of the equality study in the food industry referred to above, revealed a number of major barriers to equality. Some of the changes suggested by the women themselves included:

(1) Let women do men's and supervisors' jobs.
(2) Introduce job rotation and autonomous groups, try out women as 'foremen'.
(3) Organize trainee systems and support pioneers (i.e. the few women who have had the courage to take on a male job—truck-drivers and so on).
(4) Develop and expand further training opportunities for women.

An important theme here is the call for organizational change, for change in the management of work, and for training of various kinds. There is also a demand for greater flexibility in breaking up traditional job definitions and work requirements.

An integrated equality project should ideally fulfil two fundamental conditions:

(1) The project must be an integral part of the company's philosophy, essentially underpinning the strategic principles that steer corporate behaviour on the market. Even if an employee is 'only' engaged on making a small part of the final product, he or she should be well acquainted with the total context, including an understanding of the company's economic and market situation. Naturally this applies to employees of both sexes. However, we have already noted that women often have less opportunity that men for acquiring

knowledge about the company, which, of course, affects their ability to see their own role as meaningful and open to development.

(2) The equality project must be implemented at all levels (divided into various subprojects), and it must involve both women and men.

On such a basis work can proceed, provided that:

(1) Management and unions both genuinely support the project;
(2) Resources are allocated in the shape of competent actors and, more concretely, adequate funds for training, etc;
(3) The project is properly planned, i.e. a timetable is drawn up and progress is evaluated at various checkpoints. This last is often neglected. Many equality groups are given a budget and a rather vague goal. Then, in their enthusiasm to get started, they rush off and spend their money in all directions, often on training packages, until suddenly there are no funds left for evaluation or an assessment of what has been achieved.

We have already noted that the budgets allocated to equality projects are generally extremely tight. Even in companies where perhaps 80 per cent of the employees are women, only 20 per cent of the training budget is likely to benefit them—a result of the high relative cost of all the management training which is predominantly directed at men.

In company X, where I designed a two-year project together with management and the union, we started with a relatively simple model which we then developed to include special activities and training schemes as we assessed progress and checked how women and men, respectively, were gradually becoming more aware of the problems. The basic model consisted of three stages.

Stage 1: Diagnosis

The diagnosis was made after sending out questionnaires, holding interviews, and analysing existing personnel statistics. The idea was to discover:

(1) What jobs women and men were doing;
(2) Their wages, age, training, length of employment, and so on;
(3) The views of women and men on various issues such as promotion, leadership, etc.

Stage 2: Feedback

During this phase our intention, using a variety of methods, was to convey our picture of the situation to all the employees in the company. We found that we had to work at this imaginatively. It is not enough to write a report and send it round to all employees; different forms have to be evolved to suit different recipients. We adopted all kinds of approaches, from large staff meetings with the managing director in the chair to small informal lunches and trade union meetings. In some departments we also managed to launch network meetings, at which women in one department invited a number of female colleagues from several others for an exchange of information and experiences. Together, these mixed groups could enrich one another's interpretation and analysis of the diagnosis.

Another method was to ask the women in a department, and then the men, to discuss the diagnosis. After this the two groups were mixed, and constructive discussion arose on various aspects of the diagnosis.

Stage 3: Suggestions for action

For this stage it is difficult to recommend any general model; here the particular nature of the company and the possibilities of its situation are of paramount importance. For company X it was possible to draw up a list of relatively concrete suggestions; at the same time we were able to integrate important features of the corporate strategy to the recommended training programmes for men and women in the company. The following is a selection of the measures suggested:

(1) Job rotation on the clerical side and factory floor;
(2) Courses in economics and strategic planning and general information about the company for women at all levels;
(3) A new system of career-planning;
(4) Training in job relations and co-operation for mixed groups at all levels;
(5) Seminars for male managers on equality, women's roles, etc.;
(6) Seminars for foremen and supervisors on equality, women's roles, etc.;
(7) Joint lunches for men and women from different departments for discussions on chosen themes—some specific to the company and some more general;
(8) Further training, tailor-made for the individual (mainly for women seeking promotion).

In the company X campaign, which is still in process, our aim is to get more women into senior positions either as a result of measures within the company or by way of external recruitment, but it is impossible to say how far we will succeed. However, it is already obvious that attitudes among both men and women have changed in all parts of the company and motivation and job satisfaction have noticeably increased. In particular, there is strong evidence that knowing more about their company has enhanced the women's feeling of commitment to their jobs.

I am convinced that any company which recognizes the advantages of this kind of integrated staff development and which seriously tries to adopt these methods will ultimately find the approach also to be profitable in purely commercial terms.

Companies, after all, have to make do with the workforce to hand, and numerous studies bear witness to the strong loyalty which women in particular often feel for their employers. Thus if a company wishes to develop itself it can only benefit from developing its workforce to the full, regardless of sex.

Chapter 9

WHAT WILL THE FUTURE BRING?

In the previous chapters I have frequently emphasized that although women are still not occupying the positions which they merit, mainly because of tradition, norms, and their own and their male bosses' attitudes to their new role in working life, they are nevertheless beginning to advance to senior positions in increasing numbers in both the public and private sectors. Let us examine some of the signs on which I base my view of the future.

One important trend is connected with *education* and another with *networking* and related phenomena. Third, it seems that the growing number of *women entrepreneurs* cannot fail to have a decisive impact on women's role in the business commmunity.

9.1 EDUCATION

A common explanation of the scarcity of successful women in industry is that they lack the necessary education and training. In both Europe and the United States, however, the last ten years or so have seen considerable changes in the education of women. The number of women between the ages of 16 and 34 studying for first degrees in the United States rose between 1970 and 1978 by no less than 57 per cent, as against 16 per cent in the case of men, while the number of women engaged in postgraduate education doubled during the same period. As in Europe, most of these women students were still choosing subjects in the traditional 'women's' fields. In a major survey of women between the ages of 21 and 31 studying for first degrees in the United States in 1979 as many as 75 per cent declared a preference for some traditionally female occupation, but those planning a career in industry or business had also increased from 4 per cent 10 years earlier to 15 per cent at the time of the survey. The corresponding figures for male students were 17 per cent 10 years previously and 18 per cent in 1979. The male students envisaging a future in industry were roughly as many as they had been 10 years earlier, but there is clear evidence that more women than before are now hoping to enter industry (Adtin *et al.*, 1979). This trend is also confirmed by the number of women choosing courses in advanced economics, which is growing in both Europe (particularly in the United Kingdom and the Scandinavian countries) and in the United States, where more women are now choosing courses in economics and technological subjects generally.

However, we should look beyond the growing number of women obtaining academic qualifications and also consider the many 'on-the-job' and 'in-house'"training schemes which represent an important means whereby women can compete for advanced positions in their own companies.

Recently, the National Swedish Telecommunications Administration started a special management development programme for their women employees. The company employs about 50 000 people, almost half of them women. However, of the 2 000 managers only about 400 are women. Before the Administration started its special women's programme only about 15 per cent of all applicants for the internal leadership courses were women, and an inquiry revealed that many women would have liked to apply but were afraid of being a minority on the male-dominated in-house training schemes. 'There's a big difference being on a programme restricted to women,' one of the pioneers told me in an interview. 'I feel more secure and self-confident when I am with other women on a course than I have ever felt in mixed courses, or—worse still—when I've been the only woman in a group of 15 men, as has sometimes been the case. The courses are residential and we only go home at weekends, so during the week we can all talk about the problems of our families and children at home. It's a great comfort to know that we all share the same problems. It makes it easier to discuss personal difficulties, and that means we get to know each other better'.

Several other large Swedish companies that employ many women have also organized special women's programmes, not only for their highly educated female staff but also for secretaries and clerical personnel from lower levels in the hierarchy.

Job-rotation programmes are becoming more common, and even if a company cannot guarantee automatic advancement as regards salary and formal position for all its female employees, these provide many women with a change to test capabilities and their career ambitions.

One woman whom I interviewed after she had participated in a two-month advanced training programme (for women) at Volvo, told me:

> 'I'm sure now that I do not want a career. I passed all the tests and did pretty well during the course and they offered me a new job in the sales department as a field co-ordinator, with a higher salary and ten people under me. But thinking it over, and after discussing with my husband, I felt the right thing for me was to stay in my old job. I'm very pleased though, that I was given this opportunity. Otherwise I would probably have felt that they didn't want to give just *me* a chance, that they didn't believe in my capacity or something like that. And many of the things we learned on the course are valuable even in my present job. So my participation in the programme was certainly not wasted.'

Most of the women in the Volvo scheme did in fact switch careers or change positions after the individual consulting process that followed the in-house training programme. However, it is interesting to see that even when this kind of training does not immediately lead to any special change in position it is still an effective and efficient way of helping women to recognize their own potential and to acquire the self-confidence they so often lack. The motivational aspect is very important. Instead of having to work with a lot of frustrated women who feel they are not getting anywhere, both the company and its employees recognize that constructive thought it being given to the situation and status of the female staff.

The provision of more and better education for women in the community and the corporate world is an important trend that must affect women's chances of advancing to positions of leadership. However, in a modern industrial society technological training ranks high, and in this field women are still very scarce. Considerable efforts are being made in many European countries to encourage young girls to choose technological subjects at an early age, but very few girls or women seem to be responding to the campaigns. Sex segregation persists here, and nobody can really explain why. Of course, it is partly a question of traditions, but that cannot be all. Perhaps women do feel an innate aversion to technology. Perhaps many of them react instinctively against war, destruction and environmental pollution, and this makes them react quite strongly against all 'technological knowledge' and refrain from learning more about it because they so dislike the way much of it has been and is being used.

Let me quote an example. One woman in my Volvo study told me:

'I'm quite sure now that I don't want to be a manager here at Volvo, because I realized during the training programme that I just don't like cars. Actually I hate them. I'm a member of the environment group in my town, and we're working hard to improve our transport system and to provide a better environment for our children. It never occurred to me that my job at Volvo could conflict with my personal values. I've always thought of my work as something I have to do to support myself and my family. But when I realized that if I wanted to accept a managerial post in the company, I would have to share "their values", that I'd have to promote their products in a much more committed way that I'd had to before, then I realized it really would be best if I could find a job somewhere else. In the long run you can't separate your job from your private life. The values must agree.'

On the last count this woman is right. You cannot in the long run occupy an important position in a company whose values you do not share. However, in her attitude to cars is it sheer ignorance or naiveté that makes her oppose the industrial production of something which she knows perfectly well is important not only to her personally but also the the welfare of the country as a whole?

I cannot answer my own question. Many women do seem to argue along these lines, and their reluctance to embark on any advanced technological training appears to be connected with emotionally negative attitudes towards the state of post-industrial society in the Western world. Such emotional and attitudinal problems can only be solved by being openly admitted and honestly tackled. There is a great challenge here both for women's movements and for the establishment itself.

9.2 NETWORKING

Networking has its roots in many of the now long-established women's organizations such as Zonta International and its local associations, in Catalyst and in other international and local clubs for working women. The traditional and well-established professional women's associations have millions of members throughout the world; most of them were founded at the beginning of the century. However, networking is a fairly new phenomenon and it has its own special vitality and way of functioning. I know that networks, or groups of women gathering for special purposes but with no strict or official organizational structure, exist all over Europe and the United States and probably in other parts of the world. However, there is no way at present of discovering how large or how strong this 'movement' is in international terms,but I can say something about what has happened in Sweden over the last ten years or so. Thousands of women are coming together in various types of 'networks'. Many of them are members of established feminist organizations but they also engage in this kind of locally or occupationally based organization, whose goals can vary a great deal but which always have some connection with the problems of working women as a whole.

One of the first networks in Sweden was started in Stockholm in 1980. Following a two-day conference on Women and Leadership sponsored by one of Sweden's largest insurance companies, Trygg-Hansa, some of the women who had been involved in organizing the conference invited all the participants to an evening picnic in a large park in the centre of Stockholm.

Between 350 and 400 women came. They all wanted to be part of the new network and exchanged names and addresses. Many of them started new groups in their own towns or districts or at their place of work, and by the end of the year about 3 000 women had joined networks in this way. The goals of these networks were not (and are still not) particularly elaborate. The main purpose and the official aim was stated in rather vague terms, such as 'to encourage and help women who want to make a professional career', or 'to help and support each other whenever there is a professional problem'. Some networks, like the first one founded in 1980, have members from different professional fields, while other later groups are restricted to particular professions such as teachers, bank employees, marketing people, entrepreneurs or economists.

The network groups are mostly local and the general idea is that meetings should be held at least once a month and generally once a week. The meetings are usually held at a member's home or workplace. Usually the local networks have anything from about 10 to 30 members; the most usual membership is between 25 and 30, except in the professional groups, where there are often 100–300 members in the large cities. These groups often meet at a restaurant or a pub.

The atmosphere is open and unpretentious. A very small membership fee is generally charged and people pay for whatever food is served at the meetings. There is rarely any need to announce attendance in advance, and most groups allow women visitors without any obligation to join. This easy approach is certainly one of the reasons for the great success of networks.

Traditional organizations tend to have many rules governing the way a 'good' member should behave, but networks are *anti-hierarchical*. They are informal and open to anyone who shares their core value: support one another. Rules are kept to a minimum and administration is not allowed to cost much; members can reach one another by telephone if urgently necessary. There is not even any obligation to attend regularly; a member can simply attend after an absence of months and be as welcome as ever.

What, then, has networking to do with women in business and with their chances of making better careers for themselves?

Networking is an expression of the working woman's new identity, and a definite sign of her future progress in working life. Women need to meet one another and to exchange information about everyday life and the problems that they face. Men also need this. However, when women find themselves in completely new situations, as 'climbing the career ladder' so often means that they do, they not only find themselves in a minority but they often also lack the comfort and the vital support of other women in their daily lives. If this social need cannot be met within working hours it has to be catered for outside them.

The way in which women organize these networks testifies to a deeply felt need to share experiences and communicate them to others. It is a sign of women realizing that it can be a 'hard world out there', but that they can help one another to cope with the difficulties and the problems. Women are beginning to understand that they need to support one another if they are going to 'make it', which is why I see this trend as a positive sign.

9.3 ENTREPRENEURS

The third significant sign of women's progress in working life is the growing number of women entrepreneurs to be found in many countries. Women have a long history in this field. Even those in the developing countries, where they are in a minority in the wage-earning workforce, find ways of supporting themselves and their children as small local self-employed entrepreneurs. The expansion of the service sector has been a major factor in this development, as it is in this sector that we find and will continue to find most such small local operations.

Traditionally, women have often been found starting and owning their own businesses in agriculture, retailing, the hotel and restaurant industry, education and personal services, but now we can also see them moving into the new high-growth service areas such as financial services, computers and related fields. In the United States a quarter of all small businesses are owned by women. In Sweden the proportion is much the same, and there is clear evidence that women entrepreneurs have been increasing in number over the last ten years. Recent data on self-employed women in the United Kingdom reveals that in the last few years the number of self-employed women has increased three times as fast as that of self-employed men (*The Economist*, 14 March, 1987).

These self-employed women are having a considerable impact on overall attitudes to women in business community. They are 'Amazons', and are thus models not only for other women but even for men at different levels in economic life. They communicate locally with banks, government officials, subcontractors and employee associations, and they can prove their capacity and talent in the most recognized way, namely in turnover figures and profits. The law of business is the same for men as for women, which means that no-one can deny the success of a businesswoman reporting good results. If she succeeds, it is something she has done regardless of her sex; she represents an example of ability in the eyes of others, men and women alike.

Leah Hertz (1986) recently published a book entitled *The Business Amazons* in which she describes the lives of British and American businesswomen owning their own companies. She interviewed about 100 women whose companies:

(1) Employed at least 25 people; and
(2) Had a turnover of at least $750 000 a year.

Applying these criteria to the approximately 100 000 women owning their own businesses in Sweden we would find only a very few 'Amazons'. The important point is that, however small their businesses, these women entrepreneurs together play an important part in the overall economic growth of a country.

One of the most successful Swedish businesswomen is Margareta Wallenberg-Grundström, a role-model for many Swedish women. Her life story, and the way in which she was suddenly 'forced' into business life, is fairly typical of women entrepreneurs in many countries. The following is a summary of an interview which I recently held with her:

'Since 1966 I have been the managing director of Transform AB in Svärdsjö. Our main product is transformers of up to 70 kWA which are used by industry. The annual turnover is 7 SEK million.

How did you become an entrepreneur?
My husband started the company in 1956, but in 1966 he was killed in a car accident. No-one told me to take over the company. I became aware of the employees' apprehension about the future, and decided to run the company myself. It was an extremely painful way in which I became the managing director, despite the great 'sense of belonging' in the company.

What background did you have?
Girls' school and straight into marriage. My mother was a restauranteur in Stockholm. That was the nearest I came to entrepreneurship in my childhood. I was not totally unfamiliar with Transform when my husband died, but the technical side was beyond my ken.

What was the first thing you dealt with?
To learn the routines connected with ordering and purchasing. We had and still have about 30 employees (some part-time, others working at home). After three years I employed a technical engineer who now owns 30 per cent of the shares; I own the remainder.

What do you see as the company's assets and its problems?
The market is good; there are only 8–10 companies in this field. The company has always been like a family and still is. Here we don't have piece rates; wages are according to skill. All the problems stem from pressures imposed from above, and all the new laws that one is afraid of misinterpreting. I

fear 'VAT' and wage-earner funds, and other such complications. Before Meidner's original wage-earner fund proposal, I had already given my employees a bonus on the year's profits.

What do you do to market yourself, to get and to keep customers?
There is a regular clientele. We participate in trade fairs. I now market myself as a representative for small companies politically and in the industry organizations—I speak for small companies on the Board of the Swedish Metal Trades Employers' Association. I am active politically in various local government bodies, so as to inform officious politicians of our situation. I am a deputy member of parliament. I think it is important that small companies engage themselves politically and don't let members of parliament plan for them. It is, after all, people like us who are the experts on commerce and industry.

Do you plan to expand or to maintain your current size?
We are expanding and planning to take on new employees. With all the costs and the bureaucracy, I can understand that there are companies which choose to invest in machines rather than people. Our will to work is being undermined by the increasingly circumscribed freedom of action, and by the use of an "officialese" which, to say the least, is difficult to understand. Doesn't the government realize that a lot of small company owners have only had an elementary education?

What demands do you have on profitability? Do you pay yourself a market salary? And have you been able to do this throughout your time as an entrepreneur?
Now my salary is roughly according to the market rate, but for many years my salary was less than my employees', and

at the very beginning there were several months when the general economic situation made it impossible for me to take out any salary whatsoever.

Do you find that there is any conflict between your role as an entrepreneur and your different roles as a woman?
I wouldn't know whether it's harder being a manager and a woman or a manager and a man, as I am not a man. It's fun being a woman in a man's world. But attitudes can be irritating. All the letters that start "Dear Sir"; those times when some troublesome person insists, when speaking to me, that he wants to see my boss. As if it were impossible that I could be the boss myself. Being a single parent with three children was difficult, all the more so as I had to learn a new job at the same time. I don't want to live those years over again. Two of my children are now entrepreneurs, but I don't think any of my children plan to take over my business.

Do you think anybody can start a company, and what is your advice to a potential entrepreneur?
To manage a company is not the same as knowing everything about its products, although one must have some economic sense. I mean, you have to know how to set off the pluses against the minuses, to make decisions and stand by them, and also at times to take an unpopular stance. You can never count on being completely free at the weekend, but you do have a rich and free existence and can mould your own life. Of course it is enjoyable earning money, but there are jobs with normal working hours that are often better paid than the work of the small entrepreneur. The fear of not succeeding is not to be discounted, as it stems from your responsibility *vis-à-vis* the employees. The hardest decision to make as a manager is to give someone the sack. Add to this the general

ignorance of society about the lot of the small company. For instance, TV always looks at big business whenever industry is being discussed. And why is is almost always men who are interviewed?'

Margareta Wallenberg-Grundström is an important woman: not because she owns a particulary large company or is doing extremely well from her business but simply because she is one of the business Amazons who show us what is possible: that a woman can run her own business, and, working within established structures, can even 'change the world'. Her work as a deputy member of parliament reveals her willingness to sacrifice some of her precious spare time for a cause that she believes in.

I hope and believe that out there, in all parts of the world, there are other women like her. In the end the most important force that will help women to achieve the positions they so well deserve is the shared strength of the support they can give one another.

REFERENCES

Adtin, A., King, M., and Richardson, G. (1979). *The American Fresh-man. National Norms for Fall 1979*, UCLA.

Argyris, C. (1976). *Increasing Leadership Effectiveness*, New York: Wiley.

Argyris, C. (1982). *Reasoning, Learning and Action*, Washington, DC: Jossey-Bass.

Bem, S. *et al*. (1976). Sextyping and androgyny. *Journ. of Personality and Social Psychology*, **34**, No. 5.

Burrow, M. (1978). *Developing Women Managers—What Needs to be Done?* New York: AMACOM.

Fogarty, M., Rapoport, R., and Rapoport, N. (1971). *Sex, Career and Family*, London: Allen and Unwin.

Hall, F.S., and Hall, D.T., *The Two-Career Couple*, Reading, Mass.: Addison-Wesley.

Henning, M., and Jardin, A. (1977). *The Managerial Women*, New York: Anchor Press.

Hertz, L. (1986). *The Business Amazons*, London: André Deutch.

Humphrey, D., and Schrode, W. (1978). Decision-making profiles of female and male managers. *Business Topics*, **26**, No. 4.

Moss-Kanter, R. (1977). *Men and Women of the Corporation*, New York: Basic Books.

Rice, D. (1979). *Dual-career Marriage: Conflict and Treatment*, New York: Free Press.

141

METHODOLOGICAL
APPENDIX

THE QUESTIONNAIRE

BACKGROUND HISTORY

Prior to the presentation and planning of work concerning equality at SIDA, representatives from the various departments were gathered, for the first time on 10 September 1980. Nine of eleven departments were represented.

Since then, six annual meetings with departments' and trade union representatives for SACO/SR and SIDA-T have been held. As a result of contacts with SAMN during autumn 1980 we received information about the possibility of applying for a grant from the million Sw.kr. allocated for equality. A project group was appointed to put together an application for SAMN. In January 1981 the balanced equality group applied for a grant for a project the purpose of which was to find out how better to use the resources of the female staff, in particular, at the ministry.

The estimated cost of the project was 75 000: (Sw.kr.). In a letter dated 27 May 1981 to SIDA we received information that SIDA's application had been approved. Besides the 75 000 Sw.kr. applied for, SIDA received 3000 Sw.kr. extra for additional costs in connection with the project.

According to minutes from the meeting: 'The investigation will be carried out my means of comparing the development and rate of advancement for men and women at SIDA, and will be carried out in three stages:

(1) Collection and analysis of background material supplemented with interviews;
(2) Compilation of results and information about this;
(3) Action programme to be formed: e.g. courses and study circles.

At the end of the 1981 Gisèle Asplund attended a meeting of the project group and talked about a similar investigation she had made. We then discussed the proposal on design that had been handed to SAMN, and suggested that a few alterations in the layout be made.

Part project A

A questionnaire investigation concerning 10 people would be reviewed and analysed and a written report produced.

Part project B

A comprehensive interview investigation concerning 20–30 people would be undertaken, analysed and a written report produced.

On 28 August the quotation from Gisèle Asplund was approved. As the inquiry questions were not ready yet, the project group agreed that Gisèle Asplund would make some test interviews. Information about the layout and pursuit of the investigation was given to all staff at the department at a meeting on 16 September 1981. Gisèle Asplund took part in this meeting. As the compilation of inquiry questions took considerably longer than planned, the project group decided that the comprehensive interviews should be completed during December before the questionnaire investigation was started.

The interviews were ready in the course of December 1981, and a preliminary report was presented to the project group in January 1982. The group then decided to complement the inquiry with additional questions, including suggestions for measures.

SUMMARY

Background—some characteristics of SIDA

There are some organizational characteristics of SIDA that you have to keep in mind when judging what can obstruct or make easier measures for equality. Here are some which I think can be of interest and that have become evident from the more informal interviews I did in the beginning of the investigations.

Intensive interchange of environment
In comparison with other authorities, SIDA has intensive and 'profound' contacts with other countries and international organizations. It is obvious that the aid offices are perhaps the most important sub-organizations for SIDA staff who wish to work with aid-questions in the field. An alternative can also be to work in an international organization or as a local employee in a developing country's administration.

By duty outside 'SIDA-Sweden' the staff gain competence which can be of value for SIDA activities, but should/could be a merit to the employee in the form of new duties and advancement. Being employed in a developing country can be both a 'threat' or a 'possibility', for women in particular.

Flexibility regarding supply and demand for different services and competence
Because of the characteristics of the work, you cannot, as in many other state organizations, specialize in certain tasks too much, i.e. perhaps you do it formally, but informally the people dealing with it must be prepared to undertake new and unfamiliar tasks—as the purpose and scope of new efforts are changed.

This flexibility and suppleness which, in turn, put demands on how you handle placements, re-enterings, moves—not to mention the change in content in tasks—may involve both positive and negative effects on women's possibilities for advancement.

It is evident that the career-routes will not be as one-sided and fixed as in other organizations. But in practice it can be difficult for a woman to have that forward planning and general view which is needed to be able to foresee what kind of knowledge is advantageous to acquire as regards your career. Another risk for women is that those who have had a more qualified position than they have a formal right to, generally because a man has gone off on foreign service in a developing country, later, when he returns and because he has the right to retake his formal position, lose the work they have learnt to manage while he was away. Such experiences can be frustrating and have a negative influence on motivation.

Fewer alternatives

So far I have pointed to features of SIDA which could be said to be signs of a richness in variation and flexibility. But it may seem a paradox that SIDA at the same time is characterized by some kind of 'poorness' in alternative occupations seen through the eyes of an individual. Personnel turnover figures also indicate this. It seems to be difficult to leave SIDA and go to other organizations or companies.

If SIDA has this special feature that they who work there are especially tied to the company, you can assume that the 'internal competition' would become keener. Here the age distribution and growth plays a part too. In SIDA's case you can tell that the number of new executive posts in the near future is rather limited—an evident handicap for women.

Conclusions of the inquiries

The interview and inquiry investigations I have done show that it is far from 'equal' at SIDA. There is a great difference between men and women as regards salary and position as well as career possibilities in general. But the investigations also point to the fact that there are problems that men and women share; e.g. of communication between manager and subordinates, the lack of a feeling of appreciation, and not least that your competence is not fully utilized in your job. These are problems that can be solved by education, for example.

At the same time, it is important that the 'equality proposal', which is described in section 5 of this report, is integrated in a natural way into the personnel and organizational development of projects that are planned. Gisèle Asplund

THE INTERVIEW INVESTIGATION:

30 SIDA EMPLOYEES DESCRIBE THEIR CAREERS

The purpose of these interviews was to study how career patterns looked among women and men who have worked at least ten years at SIDA. In the beginning the intention was to interview roughly as many men and women, but after a few test interviews, we decided to increase the number of women in the sampling plan (at the expense of the number of men). The reason for this was that there turned out to be more 'career patterns' among the women.

This may see odd, but you have to think of the fact that in this context we define 'career' as changes in the job situation, and not only promotion. We learnt by the test interviews that the women who had been promoted were relatively few and that their 'patterns' were quite similar to those of the men. The women who had not been promoted, at least not for a long time, could, however, be grouped in different types of 'developmental patterns', where the potential hindrances they had faced were of many different kinds.

As the purpose of the interviews was, among other things, to try to outline the hindrances in the careers of women it seemed wise to interview a few more women than men. (This final report

150

is therefore based on interviews with 17 women as opposed to 13 men.)

The selection
The selection of those to be interviewed was done on the basis of a number of criteria. The population we wanted to interview consisted of men and women who had been working at SIDA for at least ten years. Furthermore, we wanted to have a distribution over the different departments as well as the different levels. The final selection of names of the interviewed persons was made at random from the groups we got consisting of 76 women and 46 men who had worked at SIDA ten years or more.

Method—questionnaire, etc.
I worked out a questionnaire list, which I tried on a couple of people before I carried out the 'regular' interviews. The interview technique was rather irregular and non-structured, but some standard questions were repeated, however. These concerned, i.a.:

(1) When, how and why the person interviewed had been employed by SIDA and previous working experience;
(2) Some background variables such as age, education, family and situation;
(3) A chronological description of the interviewed person's working situation at SIDA (from the year of employment until now);
(4) Job motivation and spurs;
(5) Internal or external support, positive and negative experiences;
(6) Personal hindrances, etc.;
(7) Future Prospects, etc.

The usual effective interview time was approx. one hour, but some interviews took up to $1\frac{1}{2}$ to 2 hours. I took some notes during the interviews and afterwards I wrote additional details. In order to make a comparison between men's and women's job situations easier, I have chosen to describe the result of the interviews as follows.

First, I describe the different patterns I have found for the women in the material, and after that (with the same subheading) what I found in the material for the men. Then I bring forward some characteristics in the women's and men's career patterns. Finally, I point to measures that the people interviewed have suggested in the interviews and analyse them on an organizational basis.

Choice of review sequence

The interview material consisted of 30 *individuals'* stories and, of course, there were alternative ways of choosing common headings' from such detailed and rich material. I have chosen to look at those factors which are closely related to what happens in the working environment. I have not tried, for instance, in any profound way to go into personal circumstances (such as childhood, personality, etc.) other than if these have had a direct influence on various 'career decisions'.

The headings I finally decided to use are as follows:

(a)   When, how and why you joined SIDA;
(b)   How long between different 'jumps' in your career (change of work, etc.);
(c)   Who/whom has supported/hindered you;
(d)   Level of ambition and spurs;
(e)   Important events;
(f)   The future.

Women's answers

The 17 women interviewed are divided into levels of age and position according to Table 1.

Table 1

	Younger	Older
Promoted women	4	4
Unpromoted women	5	4

The dividing line between younger and older is placed at 40. Promoted women are those with a salary range of 10 and above.

There is, as the table shows, an even spread between the different categories in the sample, but there is, of course, a greater number of women in unpromoted positions at SIDA as a whole (if you consider, i.a., wage levels) than in our sample. The purpose of our interviews benefited from the fact that we got a reasonably even spread of women in the different age groups.

In those cases where the answer pattern in some question coincides with the background grouping above I will use them. Otherwise I will comment on the individuals' background in connection with the account of the answers.

(a) When, how and why you joined SIDA

When you consider *how* most people have been recruited it has been almost exclusively through advertisements; only two women (not promoted) got their jobs through 'contacts' at SIDA and only one woman started as a 'summer temp', and got in that way. When you then consider the reasons why that person chose SIDA in particular, the characteristic feature was that 'special reasons for wanting to work at SIDA' is only quoted by five women. Among these five it is interesting to note that all of them now have been promoted (of which three are younger). The reasons these women mention are, i.a.,

'I knew all along that I wanted to work with international issues.'

'I had been living in a developing country as a child, and that promoted me to try joining SIDA.'

'I was dealing with international issues as a student, and then I took a real interest in it.'

'My father had been working at SIDA and he wanted me to try to get in as well.'

'My background is, in a manner of speaking, international. Already as a student I took an interest in politics and international issues.'

Of these five women who had specific reasons and a high level of motivation when they applied to SIDA, there is really only one who herself is disappointed with her advancement in her career. The other four are in general satisfied with their development (even if they share the dissatisfaction as regards wage level, etc. with many others in the inquiry). The majority of the women were, on the other hand, characterized by the fact that they had no specific reasons for starting at SIDA. It was more a coincidence that they noticed the advertisement. As someone said: 'In 1964–1965 you employed anyone who came along, it was incredibly easy to get a job here.'

(b) How long between different 'jumps' in your career
This issue I deal with by describing what the answers look like for the four above-mentioned age categories.

Younger promoted (4 persons)
It took about 6–7 years before these women got to working in the field. (Only one of them became an assistant after only two years of employment. In her case it happened to fit her family situation—her husband wanted to and could get a job abroad.)

All of these four women say that working abroad has been a positive and important experience, and that it has influenced their careers (they have all been out at least twice, two of them even on long stays). They all find a connection in experience from developing countries and later change of job and assignments.

During the first few years at SIDA they have been pretty quiet, but after service in a developing country, these women have changed their jobs at least twice. It is interesting to note that none of them are left in the department where they started their career. (Compare with next category!)

Younger unpromoted (5 persons)
The characteristic feature with this group of women is that no-one has been working in a developing country on any significant scale (there is, however, one exception!), but have only been attending shorter terms as stand-ins, if they have been out at all.

Some of these women, however, have changed tasks throughout the years, but not in such a way that you can speak about change of career. Nor have they 'advanced' after an average of 14 years at SIDA.

When they come to explain why things have turned out as they have, you notice that the explanations differ between the individuals. Two out of five do not wish to change their situation, i.e. they are and have been aware of the fact that alternative development routes perhaps have been available but that they have not, for family reasons and other personal reasons, wanted to venture to change their 'careers'. The other three women are, however, of a different opinion. They would very much like to study. One of them also has three years of experience in developing countries and wants to go in for more, but she says she has found opposition against this at work. What this opposition is we will deal with under (f) below.

Older unpromoted (4 persons)
The older unpromoted women share many features with the previous group, but with these 'old ones' the lack of experience of developing countries is more pronounced. Of these four women there is only one who has done service in a developing country. The other three have not and do not wish to go. Two of them have changed department, but this has not made any greater difference regarding their work or career possibilities. Only one of them has utilized the opportunity to try job rotation, and that was, according to her, 'a waste of experience'. *The most important difference* in comparison to the recent group is, after all, *unwillingness to change*. The young *want* to but cannot see how they are to go about it. *The old ones 'have settled down' and accept their situation*. There is only one of them who is dissatisfied with the development of her job situation.

Older promoted (4 persons)
The older promoted women were, on average, faster in getting out in the field than their younger colleagues. After 3–4 years they were either out in the field or were involved in large important projects that required regular travelling.

One of the three who was employed during the early 1960s has had a relatively quick advancement. (She has special training which may be the reason for her swift career development.) Of the remaining three there are two that have advanced to positions which they are satisfied with, but it was after roughly ten years of employment at SIDA that their careers speeded up in any noticeable way. One of these is, as before, very dissatisfied with her career and says she has many times been by-passed by men recruited from outside. (For further details, refer to (f) below.)

In this material it is not obvious that change of department in itself shows a connection with long-term advancement, although *there seems to be a connection between advancement and early experience of (preferably) the large direct development projects in developing countries. In combination with a couple of years in the field this seems to give the profile that is needed to be able to advance.*

(c) Who has supported/hindered you

When you look at women's answers on this issue it is important to keep in mind that every individual has her/his own image of what is really meant by support and back-up. In the interviews I noticed that the demands and expectations were very different. One woman thought: 'I have received great support from my boss.'

When we later looked into what exactly the 'support' consisted of I did not notice that there was anything exceptional in the support (moreover, it had not led to any substantial results), but there was rather the kind of keen interest, which you, as a subordinate, could expect from your boss.

It is also interesting to note that there is not a clear 'pattern' regarding which support you were used to getting and real advancement. Every woman who had been promoted (the young ones as well as the old) could at least tell of *one* person who supported her but, on the other hand, this has not led to any substantial influence on their work situation.

Among the older unpromoted, however, there is a clear pattern: the support is said (in all cases) to originate/have originated from fellow employees and not from managers or people from other units.

On the issue of support the network of contacts in general is also included. How large a contact network do you have in general? Here you can find two typical patterns:

(1) The women who have been at SIDA since the early 1960s; and
(2) The women who hold higher positions

have a considerably larger network of contacts (this is so even if they have not moved so much within the organisation).

These women are also very much aware of the influence and the status the people in their network have.

Furthermore, these women can give a good picture of SIDA's organizational background, i.e. they know how to connect external events that have influenced SIDA's developing during different times with different (influential) people's development.

Out of the group of 17 women who had been interviewed there are not more than seven who can be said to possess this valuable organizational and personal knowledge. Some of the other ten women did not seem to have reflected on the importance of possessing such knowledge. Their organizational orientation about the outside world stays within their own task and/or work group.

(d) Level of ambition and spurs
Level of ambition and spurs are shown in the analysis of the material, to be closely connected, which is why I deal with them both together.

The most striking thing is *not*, as you could expect, that *there is a clear connection between age, promotion and level of ambition.* Here we must leave the four categories we have used at an earlier stage, and instead look at a couple of other patterns. I have found in the material that it is interesting, on the one hand, to study the connection between level of ambition and your own opinion as to whether or not you have 'succeeded', and on the other, to look at the differences between those who have a high level of ambition and those who have a low one. (Of course, we are discussing the individual's level of ambition, and not any objective measurements.)

In Table 2 you can see how the 17 women are grouped.

Among the women who consider that they have a high level of ambition there are seven who think that they have succeeded. Among women with a low level of ambition, there are five who, after all, feel satisfied with their work situation. How do you explain this? It is because they have unusually low ambitions or is the adaptation to the lower level a result of an early setback? Or is it because women in common have difficulty in seeing themselves as a 'failure' and, because of that, justify their situations by saying 'I think I have come as far as I want to'?

Table 2   Connections between level of ambition; success or failure

Level of ambition	Succeeded	Failed	
High	7	3	10
Low	5	2	7
	12	5	

Another interesting group is the one which says it has (and has had) a high level of ambition but failed. The individuals in that group are able in each case to point to events that hindered them in their 'career'. The same applies to two women who say they have a low level of ambition, but still do not consider that they have reached that level.

What is interesting is that the two last-mentioned women are *young*—that may indicate that young women put greater demands on the organization. As someone expressed it: 'You must be able to succeed without giving up everything else.'

In Table 3 a compilation of how you estimate different spurs has been made against the background of how you estimated your level of ambition. (HA = ten women who have a high level of ambition: LA = 7 women with a low one. Two answers/person.)

The material is, however, too limited to attempt deeper analyses, but there are certain tendencies that are worth noting. 'Women with a high level of ambition' point more frequently to involvement in the developing countries as an important spur. (On the other hand, a contributing factor is the fact that women with a 'low level of ambition', to a greater degree, do general work and therefore do not as a rule come into direct contact with work involving help to developing countries.)

Table 3 Which spurs are most common?

Spurs	HA	LA	Mix	Total Ranking (1 = highest)
Working for developing countries	7	3	10	1
Salary	2	6	8	2
Status	2	0	2	5
Influence	5	0	5	3
Interesting tasks	3	2	5	3
Friends (social value)	1	3	4	4
Total answers	20	14		

Each interviewed person was to mention the two important spurs. The table is a reconstruction of the *most frequent spurs*.

Influence and status are factors which are mentioned in seven cases of the high level of ambition women. None of the 'low level of ambition' women mention these phenomena, which they, of course(?), feel are out of reach for them. The salary is most important for the women who have low salaries, and finally it would seem as if the value of socializing at work is evaluated more positively by the 'low level of ambition' women.

Considering all possible reservations that may exist against the material I nevertheless think that I may dare to say that women look differently upon their work situation, depending on which personal goals they have for themselves, and this in turn relates to the 'possibility of realization'—e.g. if you do not believe it possible to get more interesting tasks and more influence, you strive for other plausible spurs such as a reasonable salary and a nice atmosphere at work.

(e) Important events
The important events that women have related are, quite naturally, very varied. Each woman has her own story, including both successes and disappointments. Here follows, however, a systematic picture of the most common types of events that have been described to me.

The relationship to manager(s)
The most common reason as to whether you have experienced success or setbacks has generally had something to do with your manager(s). There are as many examples of how a good manager has been able to help a woman with difficulties as there are of a manager who has acted against a woman who wanted a change in her job situation.

The help can consist of, e.g.:

(1) Giving tips (and advice) about (and in connection with new posts) complaints, etc.;

(2) Including the person in question on trips, visits, meetings, etc.;

(3) Encouraging further education, job rotation and service in developing countries;
(4) Discussing openly the distribution of work and other organizational problems;
(5) Actively supporting in connection with re-instatement/starting a position;
(6) Talking about the person in question to colleagues, etc.

The examples of how a manager can 'stop or hinder your career' are also many and varied. It can be done by:

(1) Avoiding giving information about what is 'going on';
(2) Avoiding giving 'feedback' on efforts made;
(3) Actively supporting 'competitors', sometimes even (men) with a lower level of merit;
(4) Utilizing different kinds of discriminating behaviour (sexual harassment, etc.).

Interrupted duty
Under this heading I will summarize the problems that have been stated to occur at certain interruptions in duty, where the most usual and important seems to be:

(1) Leaving because of pregnancy;
(2) Going to and coming from work in a developing country;
(3) Job rotation.

More than 50% of the interviewed women have mentioned that they have met with problems in connection with interruptions in duty.

Or, as someone described it: 'When I returned from my maternity leave, my desk was gone—and a young chap had taken over my old job.'

There are many examples of a feeling of insecurity when you have been away—not only on maternity leave, but also when on job rotation duty. It is also obvious that this sense of insecurity applies to those who go on service in developing countries as well. It is often the case, too, that the woman feels insecure on behalf of her partner, especially if he is working outside SIDA. 'Somehow you have this feeling that you must go overseas, but at the same time you are aware of what you have, and you do not know what you will get, so it does not feel all that encouraging to sacrifice that much in order to get away.' Some testify that the deciding issue why you have been able to go out is that it fitted into the family situation—either in a negative way, i.e. you want to be away from your partner (maybe there is a divorce in mind), or in a positive one; you have a partner who wants to go abroad and who, through SIDA or the UN or a similar organization, is able to find a meaningful job. The problems with job rotation are relatively limited. But many people find that they have not had any use (measurable) of their job rotation, despite the fact that they think the others have gained in their career after job rotation. 'Others seem to be successful [give examples], but for me, well it would seem as if nobody cared about whether I achieved anything or not—I rather have less responsibility since I returned—some of my duties have been taken over by somebody else.'

There was *a great overall demand from many women that they should receive better support at the planning and pursuit of so-called interruptions in duty*. As someone expressed it: 'Sometimes you do not know what the others [in the department] think—maybe they think that I am trying to be a little more than I really am, if I start to think about doing something new—and who can I speak to then?'

In lower posts this is often a question of women's attitudes towards other women, so it must be important that these problems are brought forward and dealt with, and that you should not take it for granted that women always support each other just because they are women!

(f) The future

By means of a series of questions I tried to understand how the women had planned up to now, and how they looked to the future. It is striking how few there were who said that they planned deliberately, at least previously. (Compare with the previous section, and the reason why they started at SIDA!) Many women also expressed a half-hearted interest in planning their 'career'. 'It is no use—it is chance and luck that decide' was a common opinion. The interesting point in this case is that you do not find any difference in the material concerning those who consider themselves to have succeeded and those who do not.

Otherwise you could have thought, perhaps, that those who were successful were also those who, to a greater extent than others, planned and tried to fulfil certain goals. Nor does there seem to be any connection with age. It is just as common for young women to have a negative opinion about career planning.

The majority of the women, however, said that, given better support (from personnel administrators, managers, etc.), they would have felt it more realistic to really think about their possibilities, 'and would have been more systematic about it'. (We will return to this in the comparative section below.)

Men's answers

When we look at the men's answers it is important to remember that, as a group, men differ essentially from women. If we divide them into higher and lower posts there is a difference in content in comparison to the women's positions. Out of the 13 men we interviewed there are only two who hold lower positions than department managers. Out of the other 11, there is one young

164

man and two 'older' men who have senior positions. The spread
is shown in Table 4.

Table 4

	Younger	Older	Total
High positions	1	2	3
Low positions	4	6	10
	5	8	13

As men's duties are on a different level in comparison to women
there can be no great interest in using Table 4 as background
reference. In the analysis of the answers I have therefore split
the material only into categories of age: young (5) and old (8).

(a) When, how and why you joined SIDA
The men in this sample have, on average, been working at SIDA
longer than the women. There were only three who were not employed in the 1960s. Furthermore, the men have come to SIDA
on purpose. At least 50% were asked if they would start working at SIDA. This, of course, relates to the fact that they had
specialist/expert knowledge which was of value to SIDA. Four
of the men were tied to SIDA as consultants and were then of-
fered employment. All but one had contacts at SIDA(NIB) and
closely related organizations (e.g. the Foreign Office, the Ministry of Trade and other such establishments). Eleven men out of
13 had, during their education, already come into contact with
international issues (e.g. via students' political work). Only *one*
man said that it was 'more or less a coincidence that I happened
to come to SIDA.' The whole pattern of recruitment is totally different to that of women. (There were only five out of 17 women
who came to SIDA on purpose!) The men seem to have had a
clear picture of which 'career possibilities' were suitable for them.

Most of them could give examples of how they had been engaged at SIDA(NIB) for only 2–3 years when they had taken action in order to broaden and/or deepen their competence. More of this below.

(b) How long between different 'jumps' in your career
When it comes to *service in developing countries there emerges a special feature in the background of men.* First of all, four of them already had experience of developing countries before they came to SIDA. Second, it did not take more than 3–4 years, on average, before they were working in the field. It was about the same figure as for the 'older' promoted women, but in the male sample there was no such difference in age. Even younger men had got out relatively fast. Out of the thirteen men there are only two (both of them older) who, on the whole, have not circulated when at SIDA. The others have all advanced (including those who were employed in the 1970s).

Calculating the average time of advancement is not so very interesting, but it is nevertheless clear that the *men* are, on average (with almost only one exception), *totally satisfied with the rate at which they have advanced*. They say that they have grown with the organization and the tasks. They are also satisfied with the influence their own development has had on SIDA's growth and efficiency. From the women's answers, though, it was evident that there were only a few who saw the connection: 'Myself as a resource and SIDA's growth and efficiency.'

(c) Who has supported/hindered you
A natural consequence of the large difference between men's and women's 'career patterns' is the appreciable difference in their answers (with very few exceptions) concerning mentorship and support, motivation and spurs. All the men stress the importance and value of personal support from others (men) within and out-

side SIDA. The number of men who had no personal contacts such as these prior to being employed (recruited) were very few. It may be of even greater interest to note that it has apparently only taken 1 to 2 years before they felt they had got the right contacts. Furthermore, the men look upon it as obvious that you have to make yourself 'visible' in the organization if you want to advance. There are many men who have made themselves visible and known, not only within SIDA but also by writing (books, etc.) and by participating in a 'public' debate. Some of the men have even been able to form a 'bureaucratic expertise' (by, for example, becoming an expert in laws and agreements) and by this means making their careers without really dealing with any policy.

A great number of the men interviewed said that they had been a support to the women they had been working together with. Out of the twelve men who hold and have held positions where they can be expected to have supported women only two(!) were able to give concrete, successful examples of this.

(d) Level of ambition and spurs

I put more or less the same questions regarding level of ambition, etc. to the men as to the women. It is not possible, however, to analyse the answers of the men in the same way as those of the women (compare Table 2) as the basic conditions are so different. For example, among the 13 men only two said they had a low level of ambition, and out of these, there was only one(!) who said that he was disappointed in what he had been able to achieve. In his case it was mostly that he was dissatisfied with his salary. The other 11 men can be said to be people with a high level of ambition who considered that they had largely 'succeeded'.

A ranking list such as that presented in Table 3 can be made on the basis of the men's answers. In Table 5 the priorities of the men are shown.

167

Table 5   Which spurs are most common?
(2 answers/person)

Spurs	
Working for developing countries	11
Influence	7
Interesting tasks	3
Status	3
Friends (social value)	2
Salary	0
Total answers	26

A comparison with women's most common spurs is shown in Table 6.

Table 6   The most common spurs for men and women

Women	Men
(1) Working for developing countries	(1) Working for developing countries
(2) Salary	(2) Influence
(3) Influence	(3) Interesting tasks
(4) Interesting tasks	(4) Status
(5) Friends (social value)	(5) Friends (social value)
(6) Status	(6) Salary

The most striking difference is found in the way of regarding salary and status. No man says that the salary is a motivator while the salary for women is placed second in importance. Influence and status are considered to be more important by men and the social value (being with colleagues, etc.) at work is more important for women.

(e) Important events

In the part where I described what the women thought were essentially positive and negative factors/events it was evident that the women's examples very often concerned their relationship with their manager in some way or other.

The stories of the men are not like that. Of course, some of them discussed 'critical events' that contained a conflict with a superior, but this was not as important as it seems to be for the women. A natural explanation of this can be that the men, on the whole, have a more liberal job situation as well as the fact that they all are managers, and share important views and ideas with their own managers. Another explanation can be that men do not look upon personal relations as being so very important. No matter what the situation is in this case, almost all examples of 'critical events' in their career which men describe are related to some state of affairs which has concerned the organization in general or 'local' matters, such as '[in year xx] a change took place towards ... and then it became even more valuable to possess the kind of experience from trade and industry that I did, and I was lucky enough to ...', etc.

The only problems that men seem to share totally with women are those concerning service in developing countries.

But most of the men had been able to arrange to bring their family along. Among the older ones there are many examples of the wife being a housewife, and the greater problem for these men has been (in a few cases) the children's schooling.

There were a few examples of how the personal situation was affected by changes that service in a foreign country implies, but someone said: 'A good marriage benefits when you are out together—a bad ones grows worse ... but the latter would have shown sooner or later'.

Men do not seem to be as 'apprehensive' as women of what is

going 'to happen later on'. I tried to throw more light upon this and the answers I got indicate that men *prepare their return in a different way to women.*

Here you must consider the network of contacts and positions. Being a manager or at least known to the organization you have totally different possibilities of acquiring information about what is going on even if you happen to be (far) away from home for a longer period. Many men say, too, that they, in a manner of speaking, 'accepted to go to XX for two years against a promise of working with this and that when I return' (a higher position).

(f) The future

The common feature in men's views of their future careers was a feeling of a lack of alternatives. You feel 'stuck' at SIDA. As someones put it: 'That which we are good at—aid issues—there is only one place to work. It is possible to make an "international career" (the UN and similar organizations) but it is not all that easy, and going to industry seems very difficult.'

Almost all men were nevertheless satisfied with what they had achieved so far, even if they expressed frustration because of the lack of alternatives.

Summary of interviews

There are great differences in the career patterns shown for and women, the differences cannot be explained by education and years of service alone, but more probably relates to how consciously you have planned your career and what kind of support you receive for this by managers and from organizational policy. In practice, men seems to have advanced faster despite the fact that in many cases they have had the same kind of education as the women. As time goes by, the gap between men and women, which occurs during the first years of employment, is getting wider. On the whole, men have a better knowledge about

170

the organization they are working in. This brings with it a better network of contacts than for women, which in turn strengthens men's chances of making a career and being promoted.

THE INQUIRY INVESTIGATION

The representativeness of the sampling plans
In total (when you have considered certain kinds of drop-outs), 33 men and 65 women answered the inquiry. This was sent to 123 people, i.e. 20% of the staff, excluding employees and the aid offices (the inquiry was then sent to the next name on the list). 13 questionnaires were returned as the people in question had finished at SIDA. Out of the remaining 110 persons, 99 had answered, which corresponds to an answer percentage of 90.

Table 7   Average age in the samples for men and women

Age	Smen (%)	Pmen (%)	Sw (%)	Pw (%)
21–28	4	3	12	11
29–36	19	23	33	34
37–44	45	41	27	25
45–52	18	18	12	12
53–60	12	10	8	9
61 and over	3	4	7	8

Smen: Sample of men
Pmen: Population men
Sw: Sample of women
Pw: Population women

Regarding age and wage range the sampling test is very representative. The variations between the sampling test and the population are never greater than 4% in any separate age group (Table 7).

Other background variables

Othe background variables of interest are wage range spread over men and women (Questions 1–11).

Wage range spread over men and women

	Men (%)	Women (%)
19–20 and over	33	8
10–20	36	12
5–15	29	32
T-plan and 2–10	6	48

Women and men with academic education spread over wage range

	Men (%)	Women (%)
19–20 and over	45	17
10–20	43	21
5–15	12	28
T-plan and 2–10	0	34

The women are, on average, rather younger.

Full- and part-time service

Among men, 88% work full-time and 12% part-time. Among women, 46% work full-time and 54% part-time. The reasons for choosing part-time among women are:

Taking care of the family	70%
Original contract with the employer is a part-time contract	15%
Studies	12%
Political or social work	3%

Among men, only four work part-time. Three of them mention 'home, care' as a reason while the fourth man thinks it 'enough'.

The connection between children and part-time is not so strong for the men. Among the women there is such a connection. Roughly 50% of those who work part-time have children at home.

Length of employment at SIDA

Employment loyalty is the same for men and women. Men who have been employed more than 5 years = 64% and more than 10 years = 48%. Women who have been employed more than 5 years = 52% and women who have been employed more than 10 years = 48%. (The women are, on average, rather younger, which explains the difference.)

Earlier employment—average

	Men	Women
Govern employment	8.5 yr	2 yr
Municipal employment	3.5 yr	0.5 yr
Private employment	6.5 yr	3 yr
International employment	2.5 yr	3 months

What kind of people go on business trips?

Age	Men	Women
29–36	32.5	
37–44	2.7	2.5
45–52	2.5	1.7
53–60	6	1.3

It can be added that some people travel a great deal—perhaps seven times a year—while others do not travel at all.

Reasons for being on leave

	Men (%)	Women (%)
Investigation work	15	0
International duty	21	6
Service ao	26	26
Trade union, politics	5	0
Other work	10	6
Studies	5	16
Parental leave	10	44
Military + civil defence	5	0

The high rate of leave for studies for women, the investigation later indicates, depends on the fact that women think that education is important in order to advance. But the women are also realistic(?)—only 5% believe that there are great opportunities to advance within 5 years. The men have more confidence in the support of the manager when it comes to advancement and 18% believe that there are great possibilities of advancing within 5 years.

Questions of attitude

Further education
Fifty per cent of the men and 60% of the women find that further education has been useful in their work, to a greater or lesser extent. The others are doubtful about the effect.

	Men(%)	Women(%)
Very much	28	15
To some extent	40	47
Not at all	32	38

Roughly every third employee then finds that the manager has not been of any help at all in development.

Has your Manager actively influenced your career?
Both men and women say no to a great extent—even if this is more common in women. Forty per cent of the men say that their manager has taken initiative in order to influence actively their career, but only 28% of the women have experienced it. So 60% of the men and 72% of the women have never been encouraged by their manager to apply for a higher position.

The colleagues, however, are more active and encouraging
Sixty two per cent of the men and 60% of the women have been encouraged to apply for a higher position by a colleague.

Future career planning
What do you want to do in five year's time?
  Women have a more definite appreciation—78% know what they want to do while only 68% of the men have a definite appreciation.

Have you spoken to your manager about your future plans?
Fifty per cent of the women say yes to this, while only 20% of the men do.

Do you wish to advance at work?
Thirty two per cent of both men and women answer yes to this question. They want to supervise the work or undertake managerial positions. But 38% of the men have already obtained a managerial position which is to be compared with 16% of the women. No difference in the answers from women can be found which relates to 'present position'.

How do you assess the possibilities of advancement during the next five years?

	Men(%)	Women(%)
Great possibilities	16	5
Neither great nor small possibilities	73	25
Small possibilities	9	70

Do men support each other?
Sixty per cent of the women said yes to this, and 30% of the men.

Do women support each other?
No, said 80% of the women and roughly 70% of the men.

Should caring for your child be a merit when being employed?
Yes, think 70% of the men and 65% of the women. This is obviously a question connected to a particular generation, because older men and women have answered no.

Is the family situation a hindrance for business trips?
Yes, say 33% of the men and 27% of the women.

Is the family situation a hindrance for ao-service?
Yes, say 48% of the men and 50% of the women.

Discrimination
This question was answered by both men and women. Five *men* (15%) consider that they have been discriminated against, each in one of the following cases; a salary issue, a matter of promotion, in the assignment of meriting tasks and in treatment when serving in developing countries.

Forty out of the 65 *women* (63%) considered themselves discriminated against.

	%
Behaviour of managers and/or colleagues	45
Assignment of meriting tasks	25
Salary	15
Promotion	15

Do your feel that your work is appreciated?
Thirty-five per cent of the men and 27% of the women answer yes: 72% of the men and 63% of the women say, to some extent. Not at all, say 3% of the men and 10% of the women. Neither position nor age play a significant part in the answers.

How do your utilize knowledge in your work?
'To a great extent' almost 50% of the men say, compared with only 25% of the women. There are 8% of the women who say 'no, not at all'. No man says that.

The three most important reasons why women do not advance at the same rate as men
Women answer:

(1)   Women lack self-confidence.
(2)   Women get too little encouragement from their managers.
(3)   Men have better contacts than women.

Men answer:

(1)   Women receive too little support from home.
(2)   Women lack self-confidence.
(3)   Women are not career-minded.

Do assistants want to take charge?
Yes, say 57% of the female assistants and 60% of the male. But keep in mind that in the sample there are only five male assistants against 33 female!

Should women be recruited to leading positions?
The answer, which is almost unanimous, is yes. Ten per cent of the women say no, in particular the older generation; 5% of the men say no, but they are evenly spread over the age groups.

The two most important conditions for making a career
Men answer:

(1)   Support from your manager.
(2)   Your own determination.

Women answer:

(1)   Good education.
(2)   Your own determination.

Both men and women consider 'support from your family' as the least important.

Measures that would improve equality at SIDA
The answers have not been compared. Mention has been made as to which alternatives are important, uninteresting or bad.

Men suggest the following measures:

(1)   More opportunities for job rotation.
(2)   Changes in the work pattern (e.g. as at Lant: groups of two instructors and one assistant who are co-operating on a certain project.

(3) Better use of planning discussions.
(4) To a greater extent, look for 'up-and-coming' young women.
(5) To concentrate more on women's education.
(6) Job rotation within a department.

Women suggest the following measures:

(1) More opportunities for job rotation.
(2) Changes in the work pattern (e.g. as at Lant: groups of two instructors and one assistant who are co-operating on a certain project).
(3) To concentrate on women's education.
(4) To better utilize planning discussions.
(5) Job rotation within a department.
(6) To a greater extent, look for 'up-and-coming' young women.

The education options have been evaluated as follows (without being compared with each other). The collected answers of men and women are:

(1) Talking in a group;
(2) How to control a meeting;
(3) Training in co-operation;
(4) Presentation technique;
(5) Leadership;
(6) Informal contacts;
(7) Training your self-confidence.

However, if you rank the women's answers alone, in the order of precedence the list looks as follows:

(1) Talking in a group;
(2) How to control a meeting;
(3) Training in co-operation;

(4) Presentation technique;
(5) Leadership;
(6) Special courses;
(7) How to conduct an inquiry;
(8) Informal contacts;
(9) Training your self-confidence.

Information contacts and the power game received the comment 'what is that?' and 'that's got nothing to do with this' from many women.

The order of preference for the men looks as follows:

(1) Talking in a group;
(2) How to control a meeting;
(3) Training in co-operation;
(4) Presentation technique;
(5) Leadership;
(6) Knowledge of SIDA;
(7) Informal contacts;
(8) Training your self-confidence;
(9) Equality.

EXPERIENCES AND CONTINUED ACTIVITIES

Experiences so far
The positive experiences from equality work at SIDA, which are accounted for here, probably depend on the following;

(1) Under pressure of the staff organizations SIDA appointed a person who was going to be responsible for equality work in the autumn of 1980.

(2)   That SIDA received a grant from the 1 million Sw. kr. set aside for equality by SAMN.

In the preparatory work with the application to SAMN, and in the resultant work when money was granted, the representatives from the staff organizations have played an active part throughout the project.

There has also been a need for information about the advancement of the project, which has partly been achieved by regular meetings being held. These were held six times epr year with representatives from the different departments and the trade unions.

Another important source of information has been our staff magazine, *SIDA-INSIDE*, which has been following the SAMN project all along, but besides that, it has also raised other quetsions concenring equality. A great advantage with this way of distributing information is that it reaches a larger group of people, i.e. all SIDA staff working at aid offices as well as those who are on leave, studying, caring for their children, etc.

At meetings with representatives from the departments, a great many other ideas have emerged, e.g.:

(1)   A demand for a special equality budget;
(2)   Lunch meetings;
(3)   Pressure groups;
(4)   Purchase of literature;
(5)   A special course for female managers.

Other spin-off effects have been:

(1)   Co-opting on trial a few women to participate in the work of management during four-month periods;
(2)   That two women have participated in SIDA;s management course for high-level managers during 1982/3.

Among the concrete suggestions that emerged at the departmental meetings, the following can be noted (without order of precedence):

(1) Seminars, possible study circles about the power game and informal contacts;
(2) Special information, education, development of assistants who have taken charge;
     (a) Demands on and expectations from people in charge;
     (b) Checklist for writing memoranda;
     (c) Project handling;
     (d) Information about procedure manual;
(3) Information, education in (ADP) computing to be able to follow and influence;
(4) Work planning, changes and work organization;
(5) Establishing which women are (want to be) mentors for other women;
(6) Educating both men and women to become mentors;
(7) Debating techniques;
(8) How to make men listen. 'Voice liberation' (Asa Sahlquist);
(9) A woman from PA attending salary negotiations to protect women's interests;
(10) Training in everyday budgeting;
(11) Planning your life (for women);
(12) Making secretaries 'professionals';
(13) Training assistants in how to answer simple letters;
(14) Development services, to become familiar with new areas (outside the framework) 'person/month';
(15) Informal lunches for the staff with managers (male);
(16) Collaboration with the Foreign Office on courses for career planning;

(17) Development of managers and leading staff—generally but also departmentally, covering manager and subordinates together;

(18) A 'Project' aimed at getting secretaries and other women out on business trips, for instance, more often.

INQUIRY

(1) Sex

1	Male
2	Female

(2) Age

3	younger than 21
4	21–28
5	29–36
6	37–44
7	45–52
8	53–60
9	61 and older

(3) State highest level of education (one alternative)

10	Elementary school/comprehensive school
11	Vocational school/technical school/grammar school (2 yr)
12	People's college
13	Junior secondary school/girls' school/grammar school (3–4 yr)

14   Academic education or
     equivalent

---

(4)   Family situation

15   Married/living together
16   Single

---

(5)   Do you have children?

17   No
18   Yes
How many:

If you have answered 'yes' above

How many children do you have living at home
under the age of 7?

Answer:

How many children do you have living at home
older than 7?

Answer:

If you are single, and caring for the children,
how great a part of the care do you have?

19   100%
20   75%
21   50%
22   25%

---

(6)   Length of employment at SIDA(NIB)

23   Less than 2 yr
24   2–5 yr
25   More than 5 yr: at most, 10 yr

184

26	More than 10 yr: at most, 15 yr
27	More than 15 yr

---

(7) If you have been previously employed outside SIDA, for how many years?

28 Government employed
29 Municipally employed
30 Privately employed
31 International service

---

(8) Present wage and age group

32 T-plan
33 Fs-10
34 F3-15
35 F10-20
36 F19-20
37 F21-23
38 F23-25
39 F25 or higher

...... Wage group

---

(9) Have you *during* your employment at SIDA at any time been on full-time leave?

40 Yes
41 No

If yes, for which of the reasons specified below?

For how many months:

42 Investigation work ......
43 International service
(UN, etc.) ......

	44	Service at ao	. . . . . .
	46	Different kind of work	. . . . . .
	47	Studies	. . . . . .
	48	Parent leave + C leave for looking after child(ren)	. . . . . .
	49	Military/civil defence service	. . . . . .

(10) Are you working at present (100% = fulltime)?

    50 100%
    51 75–99%
    52 50–74%

(11) This question is only to be answered by those who work *part-time*.

Which of the reasons specified below is the *most important one* as to why you are not working full-time

    53 Domestic duties/care
    54 Another paid job
    55 Studies
    56 Union or political work
    57 Employed on half-time basis
    58 'Think it is just enough'

(12) Do you think that domestic work and care of child(ren) should be a merit when being employed?

    59 Yes
    60 No

(13) (A) Is your family situation a hindrance to your taking part in business trips?

61 Yes
62 No

(B) Is your family situation a hindrance to your training?

63 Yes
64 No

(C) If your family situation a hindrance to ao-service?

65 Yes
66 No

---

(14) How many business trips abroad have you been on during the last two years?

How many: ......

---

(15) If you have participated in any further education, has it been of any use at work?

67 To a very great extent
68 To a considerable extent
69 Hardly at all
70 Not at all

---

(16) Has your manager helped in your development by showing an interest and commenting on your job?

71 To a great extent
72 To some extent
73 Not at all

---

(17) Has any manager at SIDA ever suggested that you should apply for a more qualified post?

74 Yes
75 No

---

(18) Has a colleague at SIDA ever suggested that you
should apply for a more qualified post?

76 Yes
77 No

---

(19) Do you have any ideas about what you want to do
in five years' time?

78 Yes
79 No

---

(20) If you have answered 'yes' to question 19, have you
spoken to a manager about this?

80 Yes
81 No

---

(21) Would you like to have a supervisory or managerial
job at SIDA?

82 Yes
83 No
84 I already have such a task

---

(22) If you have answered 'yes' to question 21, how do you
consider your chances of getting a supervisory or
managerial job within the next five years?

85 Great chances
86 Small chances
87 Neither

---

(23) Do you consider that men support each other?

188

88 Yes
89 No

(24) Do you consider that women support each other?

90 Yes
91 No

(25) Has it happened that you have been discriminated against because of your sex?

92 Yes
93 No

(26) If you have answered 'yes' to question 25, has the feeling of discrimination been caused by any of the factors mentioned below?

94 A salary issue of any kind
95 Further education
96 Promotion/position
97 Assignment of meriting tasks
98 Behaviour of colleagues and/or managers
99 Service in developing countries (+ foreign cultures' attitude towards women)

(27) Do you feel appreciated for the work you do?

100 To a great extent
101 To some extent
102 Not at all

(28) To what extent do you find that your knowledge and experience are used at work

103 To a great extent
104 To some extent
105 Not at all

(29) A number of reasons are given below that are said to explain why women do not advance at the same rate as men. Tick the three most important as you see them.

106 Women do not want to advance/
are not career-minded
107 Women get too little support and
encouragement from managers
108 Women receive too little support
from home
109 Women lack self-confidence
110 Women are not noticed in the
same way as men
111 Women have better 'contacts'
than men
112 Women have more 'idols' than men

(30) This question may only be answered by *assistants.*

Do you want to take charge?

113 Yes
114 No

(31) Do you consider that women should, to a greater extent, be recruited to supervising and managerial posts at SIDA?

115 Yes
116 No

(32) Below are some circumstances that can be of
importance with regard to making a career at SIDA.
Put in order of preference from 1 to 5 which
of them you find the most important
(1 = most important, 5 the least important).

117 Informal contacts
118 Support from managers
119 Good education
120 Service at ao
121 Own determination
122 Support from your family
123 To work in the 'right department'

INDEX